BUSINESS MODELING:

The Gold Standard

Strategy
Human Resources
Finance
Operations
Project Management
Marketing

Oz Azali

About the Author

Oz Azali has accumulated thrilling experience in five nations spread across three continents. He either served as a manager or owned storefronts in information technology, tourism, fast-moving consumer goods, construction, utilities, and the military. Of these, it was as a soldier and hair salon owner that he learned the most valuable lessons in leadership and management.

His formal education includes a Master of Business Administration (MBA) degree from Cleveland State University. He holds several certifications in project management and information technology, including: Project Management Professional (PMP), Certified ScrumMaster (CSM), and Information Technology Infrastructure Library (ITIL).

Oz enjoys learning, travelling, and volunteering with his wife and children.

Foreword

How do you run a successful business?

Before I became a Common Pleas Judge, I was a business owner from 1999 through 2012. When I opened my legal practice, I asked that question often of myself. But I was alone, and left to figure out the answer to that question the best way I could. I quickly realized that knowing how to perform the subject of my business (practice law), did not translate to knowing how to manage my business for success.

Oftentimes, a business owner mistakenly believes that "in order for my business to be a success, I just have to know the subject of my business, and do it well". Oh, if it were just that simple! What I soon recognized is that regardless of the type of business that you have, whether it is selling tee shirts, making widgets, or building furniture there are certain basic principles that you must know and employ to have a successful business. The lack of these principles can have catastrophic results that can cost you money and your business.

I was elated when Oz Azali asked me to write this foreword. This book contains invaluable information that will benefit both organizational managers and business owners. This book covers everything you need to know regarding Strategy, Human Resources, Finance, Operations, and Marketing. It fills a void in existing business strategy books, and provides guidance on a multitude of subjects that go to the core of operating a company. Additionally, Mr. Azali's book provides succinct details and best business practices to help the reader avoid the many pitfalls that are out there.

Personally, I wish I had these insightful nuggets of knowledge at my disposal. This book, *Business Modeling: The Gold Standard*, provides the answer to my question, "How do you run a successful business?"

Kudos to Mr. Azali for tackling this subject matter and providing a road map for all managers and business owners to follow.

Judge Cassandra Collier-Williams

Court of Common Pleas, Cuyahoga County, Ohio

Table of Contents

Strategy 3
    Four Elements of Strategic Planning 9

Human Resources 19
    Hiring Process 20
    Performance 54

Finance 75
    Additional Funds Needed (AFN) 76
    Financial Statements 93

Operations 111
    Policy and Procedure 118
    Procurement 130
    Information Technology 150
    Project Management 155

Marketing 187
    Market Research 188
    Marketing Strategies 202
    Measuring 210

Success In Practice 215
    Operations Focused Leadership 218
    Business Plan 220

Strategy

A business starts with an idea. That idea must be rooted in reality and must lead to planning. Planning for a business is a science. Business operations, sprouting from good planning, is both an art and a science. The art of business is the gift of management. A business with neither a plan nor quality management is an exercise in futility. To stand and thrive throughout the business cycle, the business owner and management must have thoughtful planning rooted in reality and a management staff that understands methods for converting that plan into action.

Cursory Planning

Basic cursory planning starts with both mission and vision statements. The second grouping of planning consists of developing objectives, goals, and a strategy for this business. An organizational culture is important for management to shape the personality and norms of a business at the earliest root level. More detailed planning in human resources, finance, operations, and marketing are provided in later chapters.

Mission Statement

The mission statement is a concise declaration of why this organization exists. This statement, like so many other planning tasks, cannot be outsourced. A business owner cannot hire a consultant to create a reason why the business came into existence. Though the statement should be concise and meaningful, it should not take the writer hours or days to create. The proprietor should know the reason for creating the business before he/she creates it!

Below are some examples that will steer you in the right direction. There is a right way and wrong way presented for a small business engaging in clothing retail.

Correct: Our mission is to offer trendy clothing to a rural population through sustainable procurement practices that uplifts communities.

Incorrect: Our mission is to achieve $200,000 in monthly revenue.

Take time to notice the difference in the first and second statements. The difference is not simply in word selection but also throughout the entire spirit of the statements. The first, and correct, statement declares what industry the business is in and goes further to detail other important aspects of the business: 'sustainable procurement', and 'uplifts communities'. The second statement takes a much different approach.

The second statement does not give us any clue of the industry which this company operates within. The statement is more of a blind hope. It is more a goal than a mission statement. A statement must declare what the business does, and it preferably goes further into how it performs its operations and to whom it markets itself. The second, incorrect, statement is a failure for the above reasons.

Vision Statement

While the mission statement declares why that business exists, the vision statement details what the organization would like to become. This is more than a wish. This is more than fantasy. This is reality. You should be able to touch this vision with the appropriate resources and time. Use the vision statement to be bold but not delusional.

Below are vision statement examples to sharpen your skills and understand this important step in planning your successful business. Here, we use the same business as above for learning continuity.

Correct: Our vision is to gain both brand awareness and brand loyalty with the rural population within our area of operation.

Incorrect: Our vision is for most countries to wear the clothing from our physical retail store.

Let us now dissect the incorrect statement. This statement, though lofty and admirable, is not realistic. Firstly, how can individuals from 'most countries' purchase clothing from a single store? Also, the human species have a variety of tastes and fashion beliefs. For many people, clothing choices are cultural while others are dictated by religious obligation. It is not practical to state that a single retail store would serve their needs equally. For these reasons, the second statement is incorrect.

The first, correct, statement is appropriate and realistic. Each company should thrive for brand awareness and brand loyalty. Both awareness and loyalty are possible when using the marketing strategies covered later in this book. With the correct resources and the time to employ those resources, this company can obtain its stated vision.

Strategic Objectives

Objectives are the end results of your planned activities. Throughout this text, the reader is encouraged to work from top to bottom. We plan then do. We plan large cursory items before delving deeper to develop detailed plans. We make the particulars from the generals.

Objective: Becoming and remaining profitable.

The above represents a pivotal objective for most young businesses. Business objectives, like so many of the concepts presented in this book, are fluid. In business, we create living documents. As you progress through this practical text, you will find that so much of planning is measuring those plans with what actually happened. Once you have measured, you will adjust where necessary.

Strategic objectives can be both internal and external of your organization. An example of an internal objective follows:

Objective: To improve morale and retention of business staff.

This is a great objective that places one of your biggest resources to the fore. A company that values its employees is an intelligent company. A business that devalues, mistreats, and misuses its employees may eventually find itself in the business graveyard.

Develop enough objectives to round out your strategy. Keep them short and concise. Write the objectives with input from all of the leaders of the organization. And remember, your objectives should cover both the internal and external environments.

Strategy

After completing the organization's objectives, and mission and vision statements management can now begin to develop a strategy. Organizational strategy is concerned with using resources and capabilities to achieve mission and objectives. As strategy cannot be developed without an understanding of resources and capabilities, we examine what precisely is meant here.

Resources are assets. Easy right? Well there is more. Assets are both tangible and intangible. Tangible assets are physical assets: building, inventory, construction equipment, etc. Intangible assets are not as intuitive. This includes human resources (our people); but it also includes the reputation of the company and its agents, as well as technology.

Capabilities, in a sentence, is how the organization uses those above assets to achieve its mission and stated objectives. It is necessary for the business owner to consistently remember that profitability, largely, is determined by how well a company uses resources and capabilities. Capabilities play a large role in the shape and expectations of your company.

The energy that drives an organization's capabilities is resources. Employees are, in nearly every imaginable situation, the difference makers. Therefore, capabilities and resources are always connected. If one is developed while the other is ignored, operations will stall. A construction firm without equipment is bound to fail even if it hires the best people available. Likewise, that same company will be introduced to the company graveyard if it holds every piece of construction equipment without the men and women to build with them. Balance is the key for resources and capabilities.

Long-term Approach

Strategy is not a fleeting idea developed on a proverbial island. Strategy is a long-term plan developed through consensus with top management. This may seem straight forward if you are a sole proprietor. Do not be fooled! Even a sole proprietor must find a trusted ally to share ideas. A team, even if they are external of your firm, can steer your company in the right direction.

For companies with multiple employees on staff, setting the strategy of a firm can be tedious. Of course, it can be direct and reached by a unanimous decision as well. However, do not practice avoidance if setting the strategy for your firm creates disagreement. Here, disagreement is usually constructive. As the executive of the firm, instead of monitoring what employees and contributors say, monitor and facilitate the meeting. As a facilitator, ensure that the topic does not shift and that speakers, and their ideas, are respected.

Usually, the strategic plan of an organization considers the next five years. This does not place management as a fixated gargoyle sitting idly by while the company is engulfed in flames. Management always has the authority to adjust for the survivability of the company and the success of stated plans. Strategy is necessary to establish goals and make sense of objectives.

Four Elements of Strategic Planning

There are four primary elements of strategic planning: determining environmental forces, decision making, implementation, and control. Below, there is a figure that you will see throughout the remainder of the text. It is a graphic that explains the decision making on strategy and how it affects and is affected by the various environments.

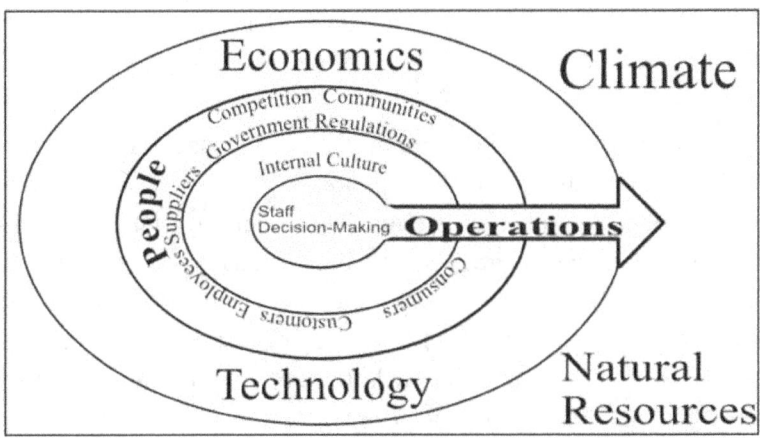

Before we dive into the meaning of the four elements of strategic planning, let us first examine the above graphic. In the inner most circle, we have the decision-making process. This does not happen in a silo, and you can see that this is encircled by other elements. Operations pushes from decision making through the other elements while also being affected by those elements. With all the planning to do, never lose sight of operations.

Culture surrounds decision making. Culture and decision making are internal. The next realm is people. People is both internal and external. Customers and suppliers are a microcosm of people, as there are internal and external customers and suppliers to consider. The next ring to consider is economic and technology. This is external and both can have either positive effects or devastating consequences on a business.

The last realm to consider is purely external: natural resources and climate. Natural resources are finite and will be of large importance to companies operating in particular industries. Climate plays a major role in the risk profile of an organization. We will cover this later in the text.

Determining Environmental Factors

It is important for the sole proprietor and the staff of medium size companies to label the factors on the above graphic. Much of the text explains the above graphic in greater detail. Simply stated, a company must know more than average about their industry. The goal of this process is not to think beyond operations or find our firm in neutral because of extensive analysis. Always keep operations in mind. It is the purpose of your mission and the background of your vision. Keep your analysis direct and do not allow it to wander into irrelevant arenas.

Decisions, Implementation, Control

With analysis completed, staff must make a decision. This is where staff earn or lose their reputation. A company led by a pussyfooter can hurt the esprit de corps of the entire organization. When analysis is complete, make a strong and forceful decision.

Implementation and control are the heart of operations. Implementation must be planned. A strategic decision to shift to a new area of operations must be planned and not winged. Once implementation has begun, staff must control and measure the plan against the actual results. Further analysis and adjustments must be made if a variance is found between the plan and the results. Together, implementation and control should be a topic in each business meeting.

Strategic planning is important to establish and reiterate the mission of an organization. It transforms objectives from dream to paths for success. An organization that does not perform strategic planning will lose focus of its objectives, will experience objective creep, and deal with more time and budget consuming issues that could have been avoided with planning. The idea to jump into operations without planning is comparable to leaving the strategic plan unfinished. Both are detrimental to the health and growth of an organization. Plan with purpose and continuously refer to plans to measure, control, and adjust.

Strategic Vision

When performing strategic planning, management must consider strategic vision. Strategic vision is the idea of what the company could be during the five-year plan. This is a great measuring tool. This is the *Better You*. Throughout the five years, the plan may be adjusted if the course to the *Better You* is becoming ineffective. A company without a strategic vision may become stagnant or confused as competition continues to evolve.

The management staff of an organization, known simply as staff, may create the strategy and the strategic vision. Yet, it is the chief executive who communicates the strategic vision with the organization and key stakeholders. Key stakeholders include employees, customers, consumers, community, and government. It is captured in the figure shown earlier in this chapter. The chief executive must be an effective communicator of the strategic vision. Later in this book, we cover communication as a vital aspect of operating a business.

Selecting a Strategy

Selecting an appropriate strategy is a five-step process. The process culminates the above explanations:

1. Identify and classify resources. State if they are tangible or intangible. State the quantity of each resource.

2. Combine all organizational strengths into capabilities. Remember that resources and capabilities survive within a delicate balance. Do not overstate strengths. Take an honest approach to this entire process.

3. Know the profit probability of each capability. As we do not lose sight of operations, neither do we lose sight of profit. Know what you expect of each capability.

4. Select a strategy that best waters the capability flower. This is where staff's ability to reach a decision by consensus instead of dictatorship is most vital. A chief executive who bullies his or her way through the decision-making process is limiting the potential of the company. Ideas should flow. Personal emotions should be

left in the parking lot. And each person who earned a seat at the table should have his or her professional opinion respected.

5. Finally, it is time to identify resource requirements. These are weaknesses. Staff should make the decision to invest in critical weaknesses for the betterment of the firm.

Below you will find two examples of how to apply the five steps of strategy. We examine both a construction company and a retail store. Let us begin with the construction company. First, take note that this book is not simply pages of texts created to make your eyes cross. Neither was this book written for you to singularly sound smart with business buzz words. This is a practical book that should be read with pen and paper in hand.

- Identifying construction resources
    - Backhoes
    - Front end loaders
    - Cranes
    - Regional reputation
    - Human capital
- Strengths as capabilities
    - Engineers able to make capable plans
    - Operators capable of constructing roads to standard

- - Strong quality assurance system
- Profitability of capabilities (when answering this internal question, think of the cost of contracting the service to an external organization. Also, consider the profits generated from revenue)
  - Cost of construction equipment rental
  - Cost of contracting civil engineer service
  - Profit of annual contracts
- Strategy choice
  - Compete for county and municipal road construction contracts
- Identify required resource as weaknesses
  - Professional project management. Organization must strengthen its project management office.
  - Office in separate region, with additional construction equipment and personnel to attract state and federal contracts.

The second example considers a retail store.

- Identifying retail resources
  - Human capital
  - Warehouse

- Forklifts
- Strengths as capabilities
    - Management of warehouse, including inbound and outbound inventory
    - Size of warehouse, as appropriate for size of revenue
- Profitability of capabilities
    - Cost of management system
    - Cost to rent space in warehouse
    - Profit of annual forecasted revenue
- Strategy choice
    - Expand internet presence for brand awareness, while focusing on fast moving consumer goods regionally
- Identify required resource as weaknesses
    - Strengthening position in supply chain by purchasing trucks for transportation of inventory
    - Acquire internal staff to manage internet presence

Find time to not simply speed read through the text but to place your company in each example.

Culture

Culture is a buzzword in many business organizations and think tanks. Culture alludes to how an organization goes about its work in achieving its strategic objects. It includes the norms, expectations, leadership style, team forming style, and other ideas commonly held by staff and employees of a company. This is quite important to establish early.

A company with a wayward culture is a company built on dysfunction. Leaders of a company not only build culture, but they also protect it. They are a shining light for both internal and external stakeholders.

A leader should thrive to develop a culture of accountability, not a culture of perfection. It is team accountability that pulls the organization forward. Individual accountability leaves gaps in performance, and justifies intense internal competition. Though competition is productive, it can become toxic at heightened levels. Instead of individual accountability with its risk of toxic competition, team accountability puts the strategic objective first and looks to accomplish goals and objectives as a cohesive unit. With this culture, there will be less gaps and less vexed employees.

Employers should look to quantify their culture and its effectiveness. A culture rooted in nepotism, rigid nonsense, and poor business practices is bound to increase the misery of employees. All employees and staff can be placed on a spectrum between satisfied and miserable. And though satisfaction and misery can have several causing factors, one of the factors can be the culture of the organization.

Implementation of Strategy

Strategy, through objectives, are implemented with goals. Goals, as we will see in the following chapter, are attained by individuals and teams. Strategy is implemented throughout the organization through three primary activities: communication, goals, and rewards tied to targets. The next chapter details how to develop a company through human resources.

Conclusion

Strategy is the barricade that protects the organization from dysfunction. Fleeting success is possible without a strategic plan; yet, long-term success is nearly impossible. Strategy begins with confidently creating both mission and vision statements for the company. Staff moves next to create strategic objectives. This is the natural progression for a company.

The company chooses a strategy that enhances its strengths. A strategy that builds the company for a brighter future or further establishes a company in its position within its industry. It is imperative for the reader to understand that the culture of an organization assists in attaining the strategic objectives. Culture can be a strength if it brings satisfaction and a weakness if it enhances misery.

Finally, we must implement our strategy. It was stated in the above text, and it will be stated in the remaining text, that we should never lose focus of operations. Operations is the entrée of business. Implementation alludes to operations. We implement strategy through people and teams with goals. The next chapter, human resources, explores both.

Human Resources

Human Resources is an integral step in putting your actions to work and achieving a strategic objective. Some students skip over human resources text and others fall asleep during such classes and courses. Please remember, that without people your ideas will usually founder and reach a wall. A wise person once stated that if you can accomplish your dreams without others then your dreams are too small. Dream big if you would like to make a difference in your family and community.

The author has had the pleasure of hosting and dining with both millionaires and billionaires. In addition to being discipled individuals, they usually cared deeply for the men and women who worked at their profitable establishments. To walk in the footsteps of the successful, you must learn the process of filling your team with qualified people and motivating them to achieve more than they believed possible.

This chapter will look at the hiring process, including job analysis, planning, recruiting, and selecting. We will also spend time to examine high performance teams, rewards, expectations, integrity, and discipline. It is imperative that you read and critically examine your personal landscape.

Before going forward, let us again look at the below figure to keep our minds in perspective.

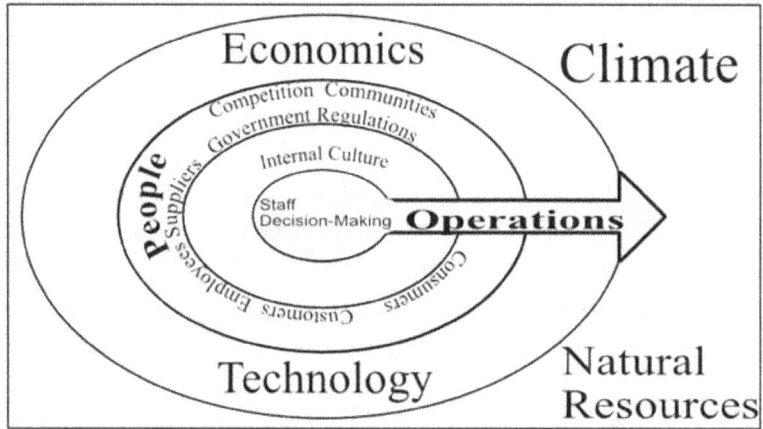

One can see in the above figure that the realm titled People includes employees. This is a critical component for success that requires your grandest attention and energy.

Hiring Process

The hiring process is unavoidable for businesses in various stages within the business cycle. Whether your company is enjoying the roller coaster of rapid growth or is a well-aged and stable company, it will need to hire individuals. How it hires and who it hires is paramount to this chapter. We contain the often-expansive hiring process into four major steps: job analysis, planning, recruiting, and selecting.

Job Analysis

When management performs a job analysis the result is justification for a position. It is the justification to hire. Throughout this process, a sole proprietor or a team of managers will collect, interpret, and report facts about a job.

For the purpose of clarity, a job is a group of positions with the exact same set of significant tasks. A task is the smallest unit of work and it occurs when an employee exerts effort for a job-related purpose. Finally, a position represents a person in the company who completes a set of tasks. It is imperative that a manager conducting a job analysis thoroughly understand the above.

Collecting Facts

The facts of a job are collected through three primary methods: survey, interview, and observation. Firstly, this is a practical text for getting your business to the next level. We will not waste time providing business school answers when reality is before us. Interviews, surveys, and observation usually require either a larger company or large resources. Perhaps even both. For many of the readers of this text, an endless research budget is not available and there are not enough individuals to observe in the organization.

Secondary Research. Take heart! There is a better way! The Internet. With this fantastic and awesome research tool at our fingertips, business leaders are now capable of gleaning secondary research to their hearts desire. But that is not pointed enough. It is how we search that makes a difference. Remember, you are hiring the personnel of your firm, so it is our astuteness that avoids disaster while proving profitable.

Research peer reviewed articles only. The article should be secured, primarily, from institutions of higher learning. This is not because they have a monopoly on thought; but rather, they have a vetting system in place that provide veracity to published works. In addition, it is more challenging to find independent peer reviewed work than it is to find it from colleges and universities.

The purpose of searching for peer reviewed work is that the work has been vetted by established professionals of your particular field or industry. If you are researching facts on a security guard job for your retail store, it is best to find your questions within the research papers published by universities. This is done by first composing a list of questions that are applicable to the job and entering the questions into a search engine supporting peer reviewed articles.

Primary Research. The primary research tools for collecting facts are the best methods for job analysis if your company is a large or medium enterprise. If not, the best method will be a combination of peer reviewed articles and primary research. There are challenges and benefits from the three methods.

Survey. A survey, or questionnaire, is efficient and quantitative. Efficiency comes as you receive (hopefully) only what you ask. Employees do not have the space to elegantly elaborate nor embellish. Surveys become quantitative as you provide a numerical weight to the answers.

The challenges to using a survey is that the current employees communicate what they believe management wants to hear. The idea that a damning survey is self-reflective and puts the employee on a bullseye is pervasive. It remains pervasive regardless of management's explanations to employees to be truthful and forthright.

Another challenge is the response rate. If a survey is optional, the participation rate falls dramatically. This is indicative of how many employees feel about surveys. A challenge and a sign of unfocused management is simply having the wrong questions asked. Questions that do not pertain to the essence of the tasks of a job are irrelevant. If the questions on the survey are poorly planned and lead to nowhere then management can expect answers that do not get them closer to hiring the best candidates possible.

Lastly, surveys have little depth. Most surveys are a combination of multiple choice and short written answers. This provides little depth as answers cannot be dissected and followed up with additional questions. Companies using surveys exclusively to collect facts may find that they have holes in their information and a handful of unanswered questions.

Interview. As a primary fact collection tool, the interview also has value and setbacks. A seasoned managerial team exploits the value while mitigating the negatives of this method. The positives of this method are strong: directed questions, specific fact-finding queries, and the depth that comes with that. As opposed to the rigidity of the survey, the interview allows for follow on questions that expand the depth of the interviewer's insight.

The interviewer may find that the scope of the interview should take a natural detour from planned questioning. It is imperative that the interviewer remember the facilitating role of this position. To facilitate, the interviewer must route the flow of the interviewee to find the answers that the interviewer requires.

Yet, there are two primary challenges with the interview. A challenge shared with the survey, is the intimidated employee. Employees, frightened of losing their position and ready to please management for favor, will many times say what they believe the interviewer wishes to hear. In this scenario, the interviewee is actually interviewing the interviewer through non-verbal communication; including body language and voice inflection.

A timid employee is easy to spot. They answer questions and gauge the reaction of the interviewer. They check fidgety hands and sighs. If an answer is deemed to have caused the interviewer discomfort or stoked disapproval, the interviewee will begin to backtrack their answers. They will explain away the bluntness of their answers and reiterate what they believe are organizationally acceptable answers. As with the timid employee completing a survey, there is little an organization can do to remove the tide of fright. One benefit of the interview over the survey, is that the interviewer can visibly notice and take note of an employee who is more concerned with remaining in management's good graces than accurately answering a series of questions.

The second set back of the interview is that it is not quantitative. The interview is largely subjective. With its fluid set of questions and many detours, it is up for the interviewer to place answers in ranking order. For the survey, each question could have a weight that ranks responses. Again, without a quantitative system, the interview can easily be pushed to the wayside as an auxiliary approach to fact finding.

Observation. Observing is quite different from both surveys and interviews. With observation primary fact collection method, the manager watches an employee at work and studies, diligently, how that job is completed. There are a couple of ways that a manager can observe work being completed. Firstly, they can arrive, unannounced, at the location where the work is being completed. Secondly, they can plan their visit to the same location.

Again, this book is not a dust collector. The reader is not to read this book and forget that operations is the heart of business. Operations is the action section of business. One element of operations is to scale our perceptions to meet our reality. In reality, the first option is a non-factor for many small and medium enterprises that operate in a small building where the executive can both see and greet the technician. This is the reality for most businesses the world over. So, in this scenario, your visit neither requires you to plan nor surprise an employee in a certain position. You can simply make a note to observe with a critical eye.

For businesses that operate in two or more geographical locations, the options above are the choices for observation. As with the other methods, there are challenges and benefits to observing your employees. The benefits include the direct firsthand knowledge of the job. The visit, especially if announced, will encourage employees to be on their best behavior while performing all essential job functions. For many veterans of the workforce who have found shortcuts, this visit will change their behavior.

The challenges of observing a position is that, like the other methods, it frightens employees. When employees see management their mind races towards dooms day. Some will believe they will be replaced or fired. Others will assume that the organization is downsizing. Regardless, allow transparency to either enter before or after the observation visit. Place your employees at ease.

In addition, irregular critical tasks will be missed in a single day observation. For example, a machinist working in a sewage pump station has a list of preventative services to complete for ensuring that the pump works in good order. However, there are daily, monthly, and quarterly services that are equally important functions of that job. So, the manager must be flexible and use common sense in making analysis from observations.

Another challenge with observations is that it is not appropriate for thinking positions. How do you observe a project managers position? Suppose that project manager is moving the project along with a software while communicating to both internal and external stakeholders. Only a robot would expect a project manager to fill an eight-hour day with such tasks. A project manager, and other managers, will spend time thinking and considering their next steps. The manager will write, draft, and rewrite communications to ensure they are efficient and accurate. How does an observation place a value on this? It does not. For thinking positions, it is best to avoid the observation and engage in an interview.

Interpret Data

The next step in performing job analysis is to interpret the data collected. First, we must verify the job title before writing the task statement. This may seem like boring garbage in the building of your awesome company, but I must stress that these steps are critical to creating the best organization possible. It may seem more critical than it is and more tedious than it must be. After you interpret the data you will report it.

The job title is important in communicating to the best qualified candidates that they should apply. There will usually be a job title associated with the position that must be verified. However, if you are starting your business this is an opportunity to create the most fitting job title. Whether you are creating the job title or verifying it, keep the title brief yet descriptive. There has been a growing trend of feel-good fluffy job titles. You may have spotted the emergence of such titles: Chief Happiness Operator, Senior People Manager, Junior Gray Space Communicator, and Project Whisperer. Though they may be cute and hip to some, it is the opinion of this author to stay away from such titles. If it is your practice to continue to use such generic and 'cool' job titles, the next section on the task statement will be doubly important to you.

The task statement is quite critical for potential job candidates. They will read this and determine whether to apply based on their personal background in both education and experience. Within this statement, use action verbs to express the essential functions of the job. A task statement must be written for each essential function. For a project manager job, an example of a task statement follows: monitor and report project status from project management software. That is concise, accurate, and clear for candidates.

It is now required that you report what you have interpreted as the final step of job analysis. Before you report, take time to reflect on both the facts that you collected and how you interpreted them. It is imperative that you are using the best data going forward.

Reporting

Reporting, as the last step for job analysis, consists of two tasks: creating both the job description and the job specification. This is the summary of the entire job analysis process and we will use work from the above steps to complete the report.

Job Description. The job description, most employees have read this before applying for a position. It focuses on the work that is expected to be accomplished. The first element is to identify the tasks, duties, and responsibilities of the job. This should be gleaned from the task statements previously created. Responsibilities can be intangible and may need to be added here.

The job description goes further to identify the miscellaneous information about the job. Next is the summary of the job. This is a short paragraph added so that employees do not get blindsided and in some litigious nations begin a lawsuit claiming that they are asked to perform tasks that were not in the description. So, it is usually good practice to end the miscellaneous statement with a general sentence stating that other associated tasks are to be completed at the discretion of the supervisor. Finally, there is a section on delineation. Simply, this consists of the task statements that were previously created.

Job Specification. The next section is job specification and though related to the description, it focuses on the candidate. It is the employer's way of weeding out the unqualified. However, the author warns organizations to be careful not to discourage applicants with very tight requirements. This section of the report should look at education, experience, knowledge, skills, abilities, and physical requirements. Yet, the company should remain flexible.

It is common to see a tradeoff with education and experience. This may appear in the following manner: four years of experience or bachelor's degree and one year of experience. Other tradeoffs are visible through numerous industries as well. One habit that organizations should avoid when creating the job specification is the use of acronyms. Yes, acronyms make the company seem like they are in the know and industry leaders. Managers often claim that if a person was truly qualified for the job, they would know the industry lingo. It is the opinion of this author that acronyms should be left by the wayside. An example of this is below.

Standard: We are looking for a PMP or CAPM PM who understands EVM to include AC, SV, and EV.

Translation (and better version): We are searching for a Project Manager who holds the Project Management Professional (PMP) or Certified Associate in Project Management (CAPM) designation who is competent in earned value management (EVM), which includes actual cost (AC), schedule variance (SV), and earned value (EV).

It is a wordier option; but, worth it. You do not want any qualified candidate to slip through because they did not understand the specification.

Human Resources Planning

The next major element of the hiring process is planning. This process consists, primarily, of the demand for and the supply of labor. Of the four steps that comprise the hiring process, it is planning and selection that are most important. Let us dig deeper to understand how best to prepare our company to reach the established strategic goals.

Demand for Labor

It is important to know how many people you will need in each job. The manager should make sense of the workload while also observing the law of diminishing returns. The law of diminishing returns means that you cannot infinitely add employees with the expectation that it will continue to increase productivity evenly. For example, if research determines that 10 janitors are sufficient to keep the facility clean, productivity will not double by having 20 janitors. There are only so many floors to sweep and mop and adding 100 janitors does not change that. Instead, things get done a bit faster, but it is not worth the cost of employing the additional janitors. Hiring for other positions follows the same logic. However, be certain that you are not using this law to justifying working an employee into an early grave. Be reasonable and manage well.

Determining the demand for labor is performed either qualitatively or quantitatively. Qualitative is subjective while quantitative has a certain value. Business schools champion quantitative over qualitative in nearly every situation. This is not necessarily the wrong answer as it is objective. However, know both and use both.

For a quantitative prediction, the manager must identify a business factor that has correlated with a demand in labor. This factor is usually sales. A manager or business owner in an operating company can use their own historical data and industry data. For businesses starting out and filling their roster, they will rely nearly exclusively on industry data. This factor will then predict what sales will be in the following accounting period.

A great example of this is the landscaping industry in the United States Midwest. The Midwest region has the privilege of experiencing all four seasons each year. During winter, the demand for landscaping falls dramatically. Sales also drops during this period. When spring arrives, sales skyrocket along with the correlated demand for labor.

For non-seasonal organizations, management must view sales per quarter during the previous year. If sales are trending up, then it will prove necessary to increase your roster. The manager must establish what sales will be in the following quarter and correlate it, as accurately as possible, to a requirement for labor. Projections and predictions always have an accuracy risk and are usually only as good as the person establishing them.

For qualitative prediction, the organization relies on the experience of staff. This is the lazy option. It is the most convenient, it is the least expensive, and if you have no employees you only need to talk with yourself. This should only be performed in an organization with many well experience employees. Used alone, it is the riskier option over the quantitative approach to labor demand prediction.

Supply of Labor

The supply of labor is the element of human resources planning that considers how many people will be available to take these jobs. This is where management begins to narrow down on who could possibly secure these jobs. It is also where a massive amount of bias can wrongly flower. As a business owner and manager, it is imperative that you consider the best candidates. Poor decision-making during this step is only escalated during the selection phase of the hiring process.

There are two areas used to determine, or estimate, the supply of labor: internal and external candidates. If you are a budding company with little or no employees, then external candidates are the only way forward during the hiring process. However, Internal candidates are considered most valuable by business orthodoxy.

The author counters the above idea with the belief that the best candidates possible are the most valuable. An organization is responsible for filling jobs with awesome employees, so the practice of posting a job on the internet or in a newspaper while only considering current employees is backward and damaging. It is also unethical for a company to post a job before the public, receive hundreds of applicants, and not consider any of them.

External Candidates. External candidates are applicants, and potential applicants, who do not currently work for that organization. Managers considering external candidates must first identify the relevant labor market. This is completed by generically finding where applicants will come from. Completing this means constraining your search by geographical location and the knowledge, skills, and abilities required to perform the job.

There are many ways to consider geographical location. Perhaps the job that you are posting is remote and there is no need to consider location other than how time zones will affect expectations. For jobs that require employees to arrive at a location to perform their tasks, managers must consider how long applicants will reasonably commute to work. Of course, this changes regionally. For example, in Cleveland a morning commute of 30 minutes or less is normal; yet, a 60 minute commute is unusual. In New York City, daily commutes ranging from 60 – 90 minutes is common and expected. Know your area.

After identifying the relevant labor market, the organization must collect stats on that market. Collect demographic information to determine the knowledge, skills, and abilities of that area. Find the unemployment rate to determine, loosely, how many may be immediately available to fill the job. The unemployment rate can mislead as those with jobs will apply as readily as the unemployed if they view a desirable vacancy.

Many organizations prefer candidates who are currently employed. This is seen directly in the experience requirement for entry level jobs. If you are thinking that an entry level job should require zero years of experience, you would be both wrong and correct. You are correct in thinking how it *should* be. And you are incorrect for not stating reality. In many industries, the required years of experience for entry level jobs continues to rise. Why are they rising? Because in many areas, the job market is saturated from young adults entering the job market and older individuals who refuse to retire for any number of reasons. This creates an environment favorable for employers. If this seems unfair, you have the opportunity as a business owner to change that reality and keep entry level positions available for the inexperienced. Think not only of the high school student or the recent college graduate but also of the homeschooling domestic spouse who spent a decade raising children. Know your labor market and be the difference.

Internal Candidates. As explained above, if you are a budding company with few employees, then internal candidates for promotion will not be realistic. For the small company, managers have only a selection of external candidates to hire for the job. Organizations large enough to promote internally are encouraged to use the Markov Analysis.

The Markov Analysis is little more than a matrix. A matrix is a dynamic chart containing fields with values determined by two inputs. This analysis provides two related pieces of information: the flow of employees within the organization and a prediction of labor supply. A sample Markov Analysis was created below:

	Data Clerk	Team Leader	Supervisor	Exit	N
Data Clerk	0.3 (6)	0.2 (4)	0.0 (0)	0.5 (10)	20
Team Leader	0.2 (3.2)	0.5 (8)	0.1 (1.6)	0.2 (3.2)	16
Supervisor	0.0 (0)	0.2 (1)	0.6 (3)	0.2 (1)	5
	9.2	13	4.6	14.2	41

The Markov Analysis seems more complex than it is. It is an intuitive tool that most readers would figure out within a few moments. It is nothing special! Let us walk through it so that you can either use it now or in the future after your business increases in both size and value.

We have three jobs in a matrix: Data Clerk, Team Leader, and Supervisor. We also have the probability of an employee leaving the employment of the company represented as Exit. N, as in any good study, represents the population, or the number of individuals in that position.

The decimal number, which could also be written as a percentage, is a probability. No worries, we will dig deeper to learn exactly of what it is a probability. The number in parenthesis next to the decimal number represents the actual number of employees within that field in relation to the population number for that job. All probabilities must equal to 1. Easy. Let's go in!

Look at the analysis, when a field represents the intersection of the same name that is the probability of stability. That is the chance, over the coming year, that an individual will be employed under the same job title. For Data Clerk, the probability of stability is 0.3 or 30%. That number multiplied by the population, 20, equals six. Of the 20 individuals now employed as Data Clerks, six of them will remain as Data Clerks in the coming year. For Team Leaders, the probability of stability is 0.5 or 50%. 50% of 16, the population of Team Leaders, equals eight. For Supervisors, there is a 60% chance of stability, this equates to three of the organization's five Supervisors retaining their positions in the next year. Stability is important when determining the internal supply of labor.

Promotion is also represented on this analysis. It is read from left to right. Instead of moving diagonally to retrieve information, you will read the chart on one row and straight across. For a Data Clerk, the chance of promotion to Team Leader is 20%. Considering a population of 20 Data Clerks, we predict that four Data Clerks will be promoted to Team Leader. On the same line, we can predict how many Data Clerks will be promoted to Supervisor: zero. For Team Leaders, the probability of promotion to Supervisor over the next year is low at 10%. For Supervisors, there is no job promotion available. We have heard of glass ceilings to describe despicable ethnicity-first promotions. Yet, in some jobs, there is no next level, the ceiling is not invisible at all. It is noticeable and will only change when the individual either changes organizations or skill sets.

Next, let us consider demotions. At this point, this analysis should be both valuable and intuitive. Demotions are rough for organizations and even rougher for individuals who must consider taking a lesser position with less income or leaving the organization. Many will remain in the company as disgruntled and vexed employees. Many times, it is best to coach through a rough patch or relieve an employee of their duty.

On the Markov Analysis, demotions are from right to left. For Data Clerks, there is no job below for demotion. For Team Leaders, they can be demoted to Data Clerk, and the probability of this occurring is 20%. For Supervisors, the probability of demotion to Team Leader is also 20%.

The next and final area to consider when predicting internal supply of labor is the exit. An exit can be an employee quitting or retiring and it can be an organization relieving someone of employment. For Data Clerks, within the next 12 months, 50% of their population will exit the organization. This percentage is greater than the probability of their promotion. Perhaps they are correlated? As a manager that is something to think about. Do not simply ponder over the best bonuses for your senior and middle managers; but, also consider the esprit de corps of non-managers. Their happiness is vital to operations and the continued sustainability of the organization. 20% of both Team Leaders and Supervisors exit the company within a year. Retention of quality employees is imperative to success. The cost and energy of training new recruits is exhausting. The answer is to develop an organization that inspires, uplifts, and builds on the diversity in background, knowledge, skills, and abilities that each person offers.

Finally, the columns are summed together. The figure beneath each job represents the supply of labor the coming year. We predict a supply of labor of nine for Data Clerks. Simply put, we will have nine Data Clerks available. If this is less than what we predicted the demand of labor is for

Data Clerks, you will know it is time to hire externally. We will have 13 Team Leaders. This data seems to communicate that either there are too many Team Leaders or not enough Data Clerks. Something needs to happen to support operations going forward. We have nearly five Supervisors for the next year. This final line is the heart of the analysis. It is your prediction for the organization's supply of labor.

The next section of the hiring process is Recruiting. It is an area, along with much of human resources, smeared with irregularities and bias. Conduct your organization with ethics and be the difference.

Human Resources Recruiting

Recruiting is the next phase within the hiring process. In short, recruiting is the marketing section of human resources. It the area where organizations attract candidates to apply for jobs. As suggested in the planning phase, the organization can either recruit internally or externally.

Internal Recruiting

Internal recruiting is considered the best option. It is considered best because the risk of bad employees diminishes greatly when you have history of their past performance. A candidate hired internally has firm specific knowledge. This is a knowledge of not only the organization but the organization's industry. This firm specific knowledge demands less training for new recruits. Of course, others have knowledge, and they put it on their resumes under experience. However, resumes are usually not vetted and if references are demanded, they are rarely contacted. This creates trust in the internal employees' ability as it has been exhibited to the firm.

A certain positive of hiring internally is the boost in motivation throughout the organization. There are few actions more inspiring than the idea that good deeds will be rewarded. An organizational culture that promotes will find a boost in productivity throughout all ranks. An organization that halts careers will discover the opposite in pitiful and distressed employees eager to either quit or retire.

A negative of recruiting internally is the lack of diversity. Here, when we speak of diversity we are not simply speaking of knowledge, skills, and abilities but also the diversity in fresh ideas. One positive listed above was firm specific knowledge. This is the other side of that coin. Massive firm specific knowledge may narrow an employee's scope of industrial reality. Internal recruits are many times blinded by the adage 'this is just how we do it here'. This can prove to be a disaster for new leadership as their ideas are stonewalled by middle managers who have traditional plans. As a business owner and manager, you must develop your company to bring diverse strategies to the business table and not simply follow the blueprint of yesteryear.

Internal recruiting also includes referrals. Employees providing referrals should consider the risk to their reputation if the organization makes a bad hire. With that warning placed to the side, referrals are an excellent way to find new quality applicants. Employees are often motivated to refer to secure any bonus attached to it. The negative aspect of lack of increased diversity is still present with referrals. This may be surprising to some. But organizations must remember that birds of a feather often flock together. A friend referred by an employee will usually have the same approach to problem solving, beliefs, and management style. Referrals, like many management decisions, have both positives and negatives.

External Recruiting

Hiring outside of the current organization's roster is the only way to fill positions for many growing companies. For companies hiring externally, the business orthodox states that the risks outweigh the reward. However, orthodoxies were put in place to be adjusted and regrouped. The primary benefit to hiring external of the organization is the increased diversity to thought that is injected. External hires, as they begin learning norms and traditions, merge and fuse those newly learned processes with the norms they carry from past experiences. This can be a bumpy road for organizations as the cultures may conflict and cause turmoil. If the organization is mature, it will smooth out and create more dynamic decisions. Employees finding themselves in this position should be patient and exercise extreme caution in voicing challenging critiques immediately. The author has seen many employees enter a company only to be exited out within a few months because of an explosive approach to changing each of the organization's perceived ills. As a business owner, this is a risk that you bargain for in hiring externally.

There are more drawbacks to external recruiting that include more training and demotivation. If a culture of promotion is motivating, then a culture of external recruiting is deflating and worrisome. Much has been written on the aging employee who looks up and finds a new manager half his age. It does not matter the qualification of the new manager, the simple optics of this is enough to shrink most giants. Worry begins to approach at the sight of the manager and the misery further takes hold as the mind begins to search for security. Many employees will begin to think that their tasks and job are at stake. They may energetically hoard tasks. They may do their best to create work gangs to oust the new employee via isolation and rumors. Job security and disappointment can pull the worst out of the best of people.

Human Resources Selection

Along with planning, selecting an applicant for hire is the most important phase of the hiring process. It is, without doubt, the most ridiculed. The selection process can spring or reroute a career. Many human resources departments have been guilty of using bias to shun out entire groups or place thresholds of precisely how many can work in the organization. The hearts of many men and women are corrupt. If you are the hiring manager or the business owner, it is imperative to remember the best talent should be selected.

When making a hiring decision, there are two primary goals: hire only qualified people and do not pass good people. Of course, we are dealing with text and rules of thumb. It is clear, that many organizations do not follow this as they hire their friends and relatives. Political and relational hires are commonplace in every country the author has visited. And no, they were not all qualified or the best of the applicant bunch. Below, I will provide a true example of this good and qualified people theory.

A candidate applied for a human resources management position. Others applied for the same job as well. He was over 50 but did not have the most experience in that field because of a late career shift. He was the least educated of all the applicants, having secured a high school diploma while the other candidates either had a master's or bachelor's degree. He could not type at a professional level expected for managers. He did not hold any professional designations or certifications in human resources. This man was selected to be the human resources manager. He was not the most qualified or best candidate. However, he was the godfather to the human resources director's three daughters. She was the hiring manager. The entire process was little more than a spectacle that wasted both organizational time and money. The interviews with the other hopeful candidates were pointless as the hiring manager knew who she would hire months ago. We often hear the phrase 'It is not what you know it is who you know.' This is little more than an excuse to not address under the table and backroom hiring practices whenever you see them. The above phrase wishes to have a norming effect on corruption, which many times sucks the life out of both individuals and communities.

The consequence of not hiring qualified people is direct, as it drains resources and causes higher turnover. Morale is also affected as political and familial hires are revealed – company secrets are difficult to maintain.

There are three factors determining how well the above two goals of selection are reached: selection rate, base rate, and the psychometric properties of selection tests.

Selection Rate

The selection rate is a simple equation of the number of individuals the organization plans to hire in a job divided by the number of applicants. For your organization, the optimal selection rate is low. A low selection rate equates to lots of applicants and few open positions. This is often known as an employer market. A hiring manager from a well-known information technology company once explained to me that the organization receives 150 applicants for each posted job. This is a 0.67% selection rate. This allows the hiring manager to liberally sift through piles of resumes and choose, hopefully, the very best candidate.

Base Rate

The base rate is another factor for hiring qualified people and not passing on great applicants. The base rate is an equation that is closely related to the selection rate. Here, the manager takes the number of qualified applicants and divides it by the total number of applicants. We will surmise that of the above 150 applicants 80 are truly qualified. With this example, our base rate equals 0.53 or 53%. The range, from 0 – 1, reflects the applicants as a group. 0 is a group with no qualified applicants. 1 is a group with no unqualified applicants. The optimal base rate is 0.50 or 50%. In our example, this information technology firm has a base rate that hovers around the ideal percentage. The base rate should be more objective than subjective. Deciding whether an applicant is qualified should connect directly with both the job specification and description previously written and released to the public.

Psychometric Properties of Selection Tests

Psychometric properties of selection tests allude to the quality of any test, or series of tests, that organizations use in forming hiring decisions. There are three common categories of human resources tests used for selecting candidates: personality, ability, and miscellaneous. Before a company releases tests to the public, they must first question the tests quality.

Reliable and Valid. Before we discover and explain the series of tests used throughout the world, we will look at what makes a test worth its weight in salt. Managers must ensure that tests are both reliable and valid. Reliability is determined by the consistency in measurement. Validity is achieved when the test measures what it claims to measure. If the test does not answer or explain what the managers are asking, then it is a runaway test and should be discarded before a baseless decision is made from its findings.

For a test to be valid, it must first be reliable. It is intuitive that a reliable test can be invalid. An invalid yet reliable test means it is consistently wrong. Reliability is also known as precision. This reliability alludes to the repeatability and reproducibility of the test. Repeatability will determine if the test is suitable for its purpose. Reproducibility considers the human aspect, and inability, to recreate the same results. Reliability is linked to validity.

Validity of a test is also known as its accuracy. This pertains to the relationship between the measured results and the planned results. If the test is not accurate it must be modified or discarded. In human resources, there are two important validities: content and criterion.

Managers must determine if the content is valid by concluding if the test adequately samples or represents the knowledge domain required for the job. This is best seen on college exams and job knowledge tests. Modify content to reach validity.

Criterion branches itself into two forms: predictive and concurrent. With predictive criterion, managers give the test to all applicants and hire based not on their score but on other qualifying factors such as education and experience. Here, the organization allows otherwise qualified employees to work before measuring their job performance. Considering job performance, the organization finally validates the test. Yes, it seems backwards to you because it is, by design, backwards. It is the best, yet most expensive, way for a company to hire the absolute best candidates regardless of test score.

Concurrent criterion leaves some poor test takers behind with its intuitive and straight forward approach to selecting candidates. Its primary advantage over the predictive approach is that an organization does not have to hire a poor performing individual to prove validity. Instead, the validity of the current workforce is examined by providing them with the test and finding correlation between score and performance. Of course, there are drawbacks with this approach. It is restricted by range. Concurrent criterion can only test the employees that are on your roster and this presents two challenges: the organization should not have any poor performers to contrast and a small company is saddled by few employees to measure. Concurrent criterion is not appropriate for budding companies with few employees. For medium and large enterprises, this can prove to be the most seamless method for validating a test.

Selection Tests

The three selection tests used most in selecting candidates are personality, ability, and a group of miscellaneous tests. As you begin to fill the roster of your organization, you will both consider and value these tests. In addition, do not be bricked in by the paradigms of business orthodoxy.

Make your own tests! Yet, always remember that the test you choose must be both reliable and valid.

Personality Tests

There are many personality tests. We will examine the two most used models. The Big 5 and the Myers Briggs models are used extensively to determine fitness of candidates to fill a specific job.

Big 5 Model. You would be wrong if you thought the Big 5 model tested your ability to name some of Africa's most widely known species. You would also be incorrect if you thought this was a test on a circus act. Instead, the Big 5 Model groups personalities into five dominate traits, grading the test takers on a scale. The five personalities are neuroticism, extroversion, openness, agreeableness, and conscientiousness.

Neuroticism is emotional stability. High scores here equate to a stressful, anxious, and worrisome applicant. A low score is the opposite: calm, cool, and collected. In a high stress job such as fire chief or utilities director, a high score would not be suitable. If there is a flood in one area and a power outage in another, the region would benefit most with a collected and cool-headed director. An antsy director, wired tight, might feel incapacitated to react to the mounting safety and health issues arising from the outage and flood.

Extroversion is a common term used throughout social dialogue. Within this personality test, we look at extroversion and how it relates to employment. When you post a job to the public, it is responsible to determine the best personality of your ideal candidate. A high score in extroversion equates to an outgoing, social, and assertive tester. This is your driver; your salesperson. When most imagine the stereotypical marketing professional and manager, they usually attach the high extroversion trait to that image. They are correct. It is a dominate trait in leadership and marketing. However, high extroversion is also the most common trait among problem employees. They can either steer or sink the ship.

Openness is an intellectual personality trait. It places the degree to which the individual is open to new experiences. A high score equates to open-mindedness, curiosity, and intelligence. For many jobs, this will not be a factor. For a waste collector, a certain amount of curiosity is required; yet, most of the job is repetitive. For thinking managerial positions, openness is imperative to the success of a team. Organizations will avoid the headache of hiring a close-minded employee who knows the answers because she has seen a similar question thirty years ago.

Agreeableness is a personality trait that should be valuable in many public-facing jobs. It measures softness, kindness, and warmth of the test taker. Though it may be valuable for jobs dealing directly for the customer, it is often seen as the least desirable for managerial jobs. It could be considered the anti-leader or anti-driver. However, when filling a roster, it is necessary to not only find the personality of the applicant but also find what personality you as the manager work best with. If you are a driver, you may enjoy working side by side with an agreeable manager.

Conscientiousness is the last of the Big 5 Model personality types. It measures reliability, dependability, and responsibility. This is the most flexible personality trait. For that reason, it is the best trait for managerial jobs. Low consciousness are problem employees. They are reckless, irrational, and petty. This is a personality trait that organizations should strongly consider.

Myers Briggs Personality Test. The Myers Briggs test is one of many tests that are used in human resources. It is a personality test that is considered weaker than the Big 5 test. It provides personalities that are binary and not on a scale. You are either an extrovert or an introvert; no gray area. This has obvious flaws and because of this we will not spend much time dissecting the test. The purpose of this section is not to steer your organization into a Big 5 Model test, but rather to push you to learning more about the tests available. Research and discover the tests that best fits your purpose.

Ability Tests

Abilities are often correlated with job performance. There are several important ability tests that we will highlight here: job knowledge, work sample, grade point average, and intelligence quotient. As business owners and managers, it is important to find limits of exception in selecting candidates. Organizations will fall short if they provide tests without boundaries. As you learn more about these tests and employ them in selecting applicants, be certain to have expectations for the test takers.

Job Knowledge Test. The job knowledge test is a basic test that most candidates should expect to complete when applying for a job. There is high validity for the test as it can truly dig into the tasks of each job. However, this test can often be a burden on the resources of an organization. Remember that each job must have its own job knowledge test. This burden on resources is only increased as many organizations contract companies to create these tests.

Work Sample Test. The work sample test is expensive and timely. Yet, if those resources are not scare in your organization, the work sample test may prove to be the best ability test. Candidates must perform the tasks in the job description before an audience that includes the hiring manager. This pressure test can either cement or expose a candidate and it is often given without notice. As an example, the author was on the hiring side of an interview for a programmer job when a coworker tossed a tablet personal computer to the applicant. This was not planned, and we were all a bit befuddled: the programmer, another manager, and I. The applicant looked at us, then the tablet, and finally to us again. My coworker gave him a task to create a report and visualize the data. The programmer was stumped. Perhaps it was the shock of a sudden unplanned task. Perhaps the programmer had a bogus resume and could not perform the task if you gave him a year. We will never know. We did not ask. With his failure to complete the task, the interview and the work sample test was over. The next applicant who walked into the room was able to complete the same task and she earned the position.

Grade Point Average. Grade point average as a test is seemingly straight forward. This is usually an ill attempt from organizations to gauge the intelligence of an applicant. There are so many issues with this that the author is unsure where to begin. First, not all institutions of higher learning have equal stature. This obviously affects performances. Other institutions have reputations that overshadow other universities. If one applicant graduated from Yale while the other from Wilberforce, the hiring manager may consider the Yale graduate a stronger candidate. The issue here is that the grade point averages were never compared. This is a general stereotype in most societies that graduates of certain universities are stronger and more intelligent applicants. Because of the many variables altering the results, the validity of using a grade point average as an ability test is low and should usually be avoided in hiring practices.

Intelligence Quotient. The intelligence quotient, or IQ, is not usually used as an ability test but it can be a strong indicator of future performance. IQ tests measure general intelligence and companies using this abilities test benefit by establishing a minimum IQ score for each job. A company hiring a janitor may set the minimum IQ at 85. The company may set the minimum for a security guard at 95. That same company may set the minimum intelligence quotient for an accountant at 115. It is intuitive to understand the results of an applicant with an IQ lower than the minimum set for the job. However, the organization faces additional risk if the applicant's IQ far exceeds the minimum. A candidate with an IQ of 120, and desperate for work, may apply for the janitor job. If the organization hires this candidate, the risk of turnover increase dramatically. As the new smart janitor becomes bored with their work, he will begin to consider more appropriate options for employment. Managers should consider IQ as an important tool when selecting candidates. Though business orthodoxy considers it to be the best indicator of performance, the experience of this author leans strongly to the work sample test as the best and most relevant abilities test.

Miscellaneous Selection Tests

There are numerous tests that fall under this category. Here, we will examine the drug test, references, and interviews. If your organization creates additional test for candidates, it must remember three things: dignity, reliability, and validity. I add dignity of the candidate to this list for managers to remember that they are choosing people and not robots, court jesters, or rappers (unless, of course, the job is for clowns and musicians). Many of us have seen application tests that require candidates to write poems. How does a poem equate to project management? It doesn't! Some of us have seen the test question asking for the candidate to name the smartest person she knows. The most peculiar question on a test is to write a single sentence that you wish you could have said to a lost family member. Creepy and intruding. It is important for organizations to respect the hiring process, which benefits the company. Respect is given by remaining classy, accountable, and only testing the things that matter to job performance.

Drug Tests. Drug tests are straight forward examinations that are usually pass or fail. The author has been part of a hiring team that placed resumes in a pile on the floor. Those resumes were in that pile not because those candidates did not have the appropriate years of experience or the applicable degrees to perform the job. That pile was developed for candidates who failed the drug test but where otherwise qualified. That pile grew day after day. Failure of a drug test is the end for an applicant's candidacy.

Drug tests are unique in that they are one of the few tests that can, or will, be given again throughout the span of employment. Organizations may test randomly or reactively as determined. Drugs in the workplace is becoming a larger norm. As drug usage rips the United States, many rural and small towns are experiencing shortages in labor supply. Large cities are better at withstanding this scourge because of their larger populations of qualified applicants. Continuous drug testing is important for ensuring that your workforce is sober when performing their tasks.

A drugged and incoherent employee spreads risk to many stakeholders: the organization, coworkers, customers, vendors, and themselves. As a business owner or manager, it is necessary to form a random drug test for anyone operating machinery or a vehicle. Imagine a woman driving a 20-ton garbage truck under the influence of a psychotropic drug. The cost of the drug test is far less than the cost of litigation for hurting a person or damaging their property.

For applicants who fail a drug test, the result is swift – not hired. For employees who fail a random or reactionary drug test, the result is more complicated. As this section deals with the selection phase of the hiring process, the author will only advise that the business owner and manager consult the law of their area of operations. Some nations treat drug abuse as a disease. Others treat individuals who are chemically dependent as pests. Organizations should know the applicable law and develop company policy to address this issue. Drugs are prevalent in nearly all societies regardless of geographical location, wealth, gender, or any other factor. It is how organization's respond to challenges that shape their culture and build their reputation.

References. The reference. Most have been asked to provide them. Most remember the anxiety as you experienced when you asked the professor or past supervisor to be a reference. In some organizations, it ends there. An applicant lists a name on the last page of their resume, submits it, and hopes for the best. Other organizations can require applicants to develop this into a recommendation.

Organizations can demand recommendations from several references. Applicants might become unsure of themselves as the company demands that recommendations be submitted directly from the reference to the firm. It may surprise many to find that many references are not contacted and most recommendation letters are not read.

Both the reference and the recommendation are nearly worthless, and many organizations know this; but, still demand them. A hiring manager, who admittedly did not call references or read recommendations, stated that she still demanded them so candidates can show resourcefulness. Organizations are usually not concerned with references and recommendations because most candidates are careful to only select individuals who hold them in high regard. This obviously places an asterisk on this abilities test.

Interviews. The interview is the most common selection test and for many organizations it is the most important. Extroverts do well in interviews and hiring managers are strongly advised to separate wide smiles from exact plans and continuous talking from substance. For organizations, the nightmare of not hiring a good employee should be matched by the tremor of employing an underqualified individual. Many people talk their way into positions that they cannot handle. Of course, this is not the fault of these ambitious candidates. The blame rests solely on the star struck organizations who hire them.

The author has interviewed candidates who leaped upon the table singing their resume, who answered the first question by providing the details of their political connection, and women who wore transparent clothing. In each instant, it is imperative that the hiring manager remains professional and in control. The interviewer must never allow a runaway interview. The hiring manager must structure the interview with job related questions while remaining flexible enough to allow the personality and abilities of the candidate to become apparent.

The hiring process is a critical step in building a business that is sustained with good people. An organization cannot have job growth without hiring qualified individuals who will implement their strategic objectives. The biggest variable contributing to the failure of human resources is corruption. Corruption can take many forms throughout society; yet, it appears continuously in the hiring process. Organizations choosing to hire based on skin tone, ethnicity, nationality, country of origin, gender, and family relationships is destructive and costly. As a business owner and manager, it is key that you hire only the best while ignoring the external forces pressuring you to make baseless decisions.

Performance

Now your organization has a team with their collective eyes fastened upon the strategic objectives and goals. Your team, through processes, have the power to either build or destroy the company. In the following pages, we will look at the makeup of high-performing teams, expectations, and integrity. Bringing together qualified individuals is not the finish line in growing a company.

High Performance

This phrase has received much attention throughout most business circles. The term is intuitive enough; yet, when explaining high performance teams many seem to believe that the behaviors simply 'happen'. They do not. High performance teams require training, great management, and time.

Training

A manager once laid a training plan on the desk of his executive involving three of his subordinate employees. The executive looked at the plan and the benefits of them to the company. The executive looked up and said, 'We do not have a retention agreement for the employees. What if we pay to train them and they leave?' The witty manager told the executive 'What if we don't train them and they stay!'

Training is key to most high-performance teams. Training is important even if the team has more degrees than a thermometer. Formal education is not the end of knowledge and most institutions recognize the gaps in the curriculum. Technical team members will benefit from training on the latest technology. Newly appointed supervisors without a formal education will find basic supervision courses useful. Training should be task and job specific. A quality manager finds the weaknesses and strengths in team members and creates a training plan accordingly.

High performance is as much an individual behavior as it is an environment. The organizational culture creates and sustains high performance by developing challenging work, holding employees accountable, and remaining open to suggestions. Challenging work becomes increasingly important as the individual grows in skill. A laborer may embrace a week of little work. A project manager without work may get bored. An organization uses challenging work to keep employees fully engaged and to grow the company.

Employees, at all levels of the company, must be held to account. Accountability increases performance by incentivizing quality work. A team, knowing that poor work is not accepted, will produce better assignments. It is, at its primal level, a survival tactic. There is a large United States Corporation that annually fires the bottom performing 10% of the company. This is a bit extreme. This can create a cannibalizing culture of managers not wanting to be the bottom 10, which can tarnish trust and create cliques. There are certain ills with this extreme management decision. However, the idea of incentivizing quality work could not be more overstated and pronounced. Either you perform or you leave. This creates high performing accountable teams striving for greater tomorrows.

The opposite is true in many government work environments. First, let us state the obvious: government workers are usually weighted down to the ground with mounting work that never ceases. There are operations and capital improvement projects, and in many cases endless emergencies. All of this is completed with limited managerial staff. Yet, there is also the stereotypical side of government that seems to be more widely known: the manager who is burnt out, does nothing, and waits for retirement. Governments have a harder time removing poor performing employees and the result is mediocre teams with some motivated employees and other stalling employees. If your organization is going to reach beyond the vision of your dreams, you must either motivate employees or remove them!

Managing for Performance

We alluded to managing performance above. It is a careful balance of care, abilities, and facilitation. If your organization made selections of quality candidates, high performance will be within the grasps of each of them. Managers place individuals over tasks based on their strengths. It sounds simply. It is. However, individuals are not placed where they can best help the company for various reasons. Perhaps an employee developed a monopoly on tasks and the manager does not want to create a wave. That employee could have mediocre performance and a 'But this is how we always do it' attitude. The cowardly manager and the poor performing employee could make an eager employee lose drive. Good management is bold. It is willing to be cursed and despised in protection of the bigger picture.

Managers must facilitate meetings and not necessarily drive them. I know of no individual who enjoys being talk at. Managers must get off their stump, take a pause from simply relaying communications from executives, and allow their subordinates and colleagues the time to figure it out and flower. A diverse team entering a room with different experiences and knowledge fields will differ and argue and yell and shout and work through it and plan and succeed together. A manager that races to end an argument and hush a loud room is muffling greatness. Managers must know that there is greatness inside of each employee and it shines and expresses itself, not when caged but when liberated.

Facilitate meetings using methods such as nominal group technique or charrette. A friend of the author, Dr. Natasha Palesa Mothapo of South Africa, co-wrote a great article on the benefits of charettes in business: 3-Step Charrette. In the article, the authors examined the charrette and compared the decision-making tool to other similar tools. Charettes, and other tools, allow teams to solve challenges in an organic way. Managers must find creative avenues to reach the best possible solution to whatever challenge is facing the company.

Management is such a critical step in raising high performance teams. Management has the power to either shock an individual into a pigeonhole, frightened that a suggestion to change a process could draw wrath or it can empower an employee to improve the organization. Jealous management is a systemic problem that attempts to stomp out the embers of any promising employee that they perceive has either more knowledge or vibrancy. Senior management must punish this bullying management if, of course, they are not part of the problem. If management continues to bully its brightest stars, they will find that motivation leaks from their company like a tire with a hole in it. In fact, every promising employee will search desperately for better opportunities and leave as soon as the best offer arises.

Time

There is little in the business world as precious and as powerful as time. It takes time to reasonably expect great results from a startup. It takes time to determine if your passion is a business or a hobby. It also takes time for teams to mesh and find a groove. The groove is the area of high performance. The idea of time as correlated with performance is captured by the five phases of group development.

The five stages of group development include gathering, learning, establishing, delivering, and dispersing. Gathering begins with the hiring process described in detail earlier in this chapter. It goes beyond onboarding and training as new employees are placed on teams. Existing employees also adjust; not only with incoming personnel but also with the changing dynamics of operations and projects. Gathering is therefore the coming together of new and existing employees in groups to accomplish stated tasks and goals. It is an intuitive commencement of differing personalities with various backgrounds and it often leads to learning.

The learning phase of this group development is captured by individuals finding how they fit into the team. Team members interact in various ways to the work and they begin learning the quirks of the others. In this phase of team development, arguments and disagreements are common. The leader of the team must allow and facilitate arguments as the basis for reaching consensus. Teams with intelligent members should expect more disagreements as personalities find ways to mesh.

Members also learn more about what is expected of them. A project team may have a cursory understanding of the project statement of work; yet, in this stage the details of the project plan is unveiled. They do the unveiling. The team is guided by executives; however, they are often accountable to the details. In operations, the learning stage is critical to achieving strategic objectives.

Within the learning phase, members plan work and establish 'lanes' for members. Lanes are best on roadways. These lanes, or silos as they are sometimes called, are tasks that employees decide are best completed by one individual. They are usually softly established but fiercely guarded. Job tasks are assigned by the organization, while lanes are captured by employees. Silos are territorial and performing tasks within another employee's lane without consent can lead to shunning. Lanes are inevitable and organizations should monitor fair play without wasting energy attempting to stop them. They will spring up again and again like a forgotten acacia seed. With the team having learned of themselves and what is expected of them, they will begin to establish a set of both formal and informal rules of conduct.

The establishing phase of team development is both written and verbal. The group will benefit by writing down and signing rules of participation. Rules can include the mode of communication used such as emails and telephone calls but not faxes and letters. Rules should also detail how meetings must be conducted and what is acceptable language. This should highlight that berating another's ideas as stupid or ridiculous is unacceptable. This provision thwarts bullying, which is a cancer to a team's progress. Other rules that could be agreed to, include how often meetings will occur, who is the point of contact for external communications within the organization, timeline for work to be completed, how disputes will be resolved, and how to remove non-performing members. If the group is performing operations and not a project, it will usually not have the authority to remove members from the organization. The written agreement must be signed by each member. This signing is not to make it legally binding as some may conclude.

Instead, it is to hold the individual accountable. Most people throughout the world hold their reputation in high esteem and care to protect it. Showing an employee his own signature can have magical affects for his performance and behavior.

Rules are also verbal and informal. This relates to lanes as described above. An informal rule is anything not stated in writing. These informal or verbal practices can be not eating in a meeting or not reheating yesterday's fish dinner in the cafeteria. Informal rules may seem unimportant, but they can cause discomfort and feuds between members. Arguments have occurred over the use of microwaves, mobile phone usage in meetings, and response times to emails. Remember, if the rule is a deal breaker, put it in writing. Yet, If the rule would make team-life better, keep it informal.

The delivering phase is the tip of the iceberg in group development. The iceberg is mostly underwater and what a terrestrial being sees is the lesser part of the mass. Most of the time spent by groups is clustered in the first three phases: gather, learn, and establish. We know that teams often procrastinate. They talk and talk and finally do. Teams with highly educated members are at risk for greater procrastination. There is empirical research that proves that as individuals become more skilled and educated, their work slows. The two are correlated. Of course, this is because they are spending more time considering how to take the next step. This is great until it hinders performance as the work trickles. Team leaders and managers must push work schedules as a vital element of operations. Delivery is not planning. Delivery is performing operations.

As members enter and exit dynamic teams, these phases will occur again and again. Managers should expect these phases and facilitate their development. The group will deliver either a product, service, or result and the manager is responsible for controlling the quality. We will go deeper into quality control in the operations chapter. For now, remember, if quality control is not performed then your operations are amateurish and in desperate need of greater management.

The final phase of group development is dispersing. After the team delivers, it may go its separate ways. If it is operations, then it will go from delivery to delivery without dispersing. If it is a project team then it may go from project to project or disperse after a single project. If the organization hires a contractor, then the contractor will leave after the stated time or result is achieved in the agreement. Therefore, this phase is dependent on other factors. Yet, if the team does disperse, a celebration is due. Organizations should celebrate its accomplishments and groups are no different. Dispersing after a successful endeavor is a great cause for a party!

Time is an unrenewable resource. It is here then it is gone. For high performing teams, time is structured by the five phases of group development. The phases are complex in how they manifest; yet, with structured management and guided facilitation, they culminate with superb delivery of products, services, and results. These phases are relevant for small and large organizations and in any industry. Time is an important factor for achieving the high-performance team.

Expectations

Expectations of the organization should be captured in the organization and individual goals. This is yet another framework that allows management to delegate tasks and responsibility throughout the organization. For an organization to increase morale, rewards and progressive discipline must be hinged to expectations.

Rewards

It does not need to be stated that discipline is connected to expectations. Each organization knows this. The employees know this when they apply for the job after reading the specifications and description. Unfortunately, rewards do not share the same organizational buy-in. If and how rewards are distributed throughout the company shapes organizational culture. Rewards include commission, merit-based bonus, tenure-based bonus, and other non-monetary rewards.

Commission. This is the most common reward system. It is fair, often negotiated during the hiring process, and relied upon by the employee. Commission is seen nearly exclusively in sales jobs. As the salesperson earns customers, the organization rewards this behavior with commission. This is a contracted agreement and both the employee and employer must uphold their end to avoid litigation.

Merit-Based Bonus. The merit-based reward is similar to the commission, yet this reward is not always in a contract. This bonus can be loosely tied to performance or specifically correlated with a measure. The author remembers a hard-working accountant who waited desperately for her bonus at the end of the year to remodel her home. She had worked for this organization for years and had grown to expect her end of year bonus. The organization rented a large conference room and invited their employees to attend. Everyone on the roster arrived at this end of year conference. Each expecting a bonus like the years before. The CEO held forth for an hour before envelops were passed to the employees. They tore into them only to find a thank you card. Profit was down and the organization could not give bonuses this year. The accountant used this as motivation to raise her accounting company and within a year, she retired from her job. Staff should establish expectations for rewards to avoid uncomfortable surprises.

The merit-based bonus may also be distributed when an employee reaches a certain target. The bonus can be dependent on revenue, profit, or share price for publicly traded companies. The bonus is usually a percentage of annual salary and can range from 1% - 100%. A New York executive recently shared his merit-based bonus system at his organization. If revenue hits predetermined heights, the executive receives 100% of his salary as a bonus. Not bad, considering he earns $300,000 a year. This reward system contributes to considerable motivation of employees.

Tenure-Based Bonus. Tenure-based bonuses is a less motivating reward system. These bonuses reward employees for not quitting and moving to a new organization. It has no correlation to job performance. Organizations should be careful when deciding to use these bonuses as they can sap motivation away from new employees. If recently onboarded employees find that the company rewards tenure and not merit, the attitude and verve of the workforce may change. The author has worked in an organization that distributed these bonuses. The first bonuses were distributed after five years on the job. The bonuses were not a percentage of salary and were identical for everyone who reached that point. The bonus amount increased every five years until it maxed out at a pathetic $750 during year 20. In such a system, new managers receiving nothing for their labor had to witness customer service representatives and janitors taking home a bonus. It is as upside down as it appears.

Tenure-based bonus systems work well for company that want to give something but cannot give much. By first distributing the bonus at five years, employers are free from compensating transient employees. Statistics show that most employees remain with a single employer for about four years. This makes the tenure-based bonus system cheaper than the merit-based system. Companies should analyze how much they are willing to spend to entice and retain talent.

Non-Monetary Rewards. Non-monetary rewards include such titles as Employee of the Year and certificates of appreciations. The most ambitious employees will seek to be the Employee of the Month so that they can record it on their resume. Many seasoned professionals simply do not care about these titles. Seasoned and accomplished professionals have quality credentials that cast a daunting shadow on a certificate of appreciation. When possible, it is never best to employ this reward system in solitary. Organizations and managers must use rewards to boost performance and morale. The non-monetary reward system does not always accomplish this. Of course, this could be a good start for young companies that do not have the cash to offer monetary bonuses.

Discipline

Expectations that are not met must lead to discipline. This task is either a joy or a pain depending on the depravity of the manager. Organizations are littered with managers and supervisors who relish the opportunity to put paperwork on subordinates. Perhaps these supervisors believe that their stature within the company will be rewarded by harshly disciplining others. This view is destructive, and organizations must tackle the notion that this will lead to promotion. Discipline is not a tool for career growth, it is the necessary requirement for expectations left unmet.

Coaching. Before discipline meets paper, and certainly before dismissal, companies should embrace coaching. We must preface this by stating that dangerous and illegal behavior require harsh discipline and dismissal. An employee who threatens another may experience progressive discipline while an employee who slaps an employee during a disagreement must be removed. Most discipline is required for poor performance and minor offenses that can be resolved through coaching.

Coaching is not a simple verbal warning. It is not a verbal correction either. Coaching is an organization's calculated step toward resolving an existing issue. Coaching is not impromptu. It requires time allotted on the schedule for the supervisor to readjust behavior and performance by stating what the organization expects of the employee. The supervisor dissects a task and walks through the performance of the task. The supervisor may also recommend additional training for the employee.

Paperwork. After coaching, a more robotic progressive discipline is the way forward. Parenthetically, some organizations can go in and out of coaching for months in a leisure attempt to correct behavior and performance. Other firms that do not embrace coaching may go directly into paperwork. Much of how an organization decides to discipline is part of its unwritten culture.

Progressive discipline must be established before it is used. There are no wrong answers when creating your progressive discipline. The only trouble that organizations find themselves in is when it is applied to some but not all. This is a human error that must be avoided. Supervisors and managers have favorite employees and they have others who they wish would quit in the afternoon. They must keep this bias to themselves and not allow it to leak into the disciplining process.

Progressive discipline varies. It can be a five-step process or less. Regardless of how many steps, continued poor performance or behavior will lead to dismissal. Progressive discipline systems reset after a period, usually within 18 months from step one with good behavior.

An example of a modifiable progressive system follows:

1. Verbal warning – A verbal communication reiterating the progressive system.

2. Written warning – A more serious approach to problem solving. The organization is warning the employee that the next step is non-paid time off. Each step is intertwined with coaching. Quality management is not racing to steps three through five. The best managers are simply trying to correct poor behavior and performance.

3. Two-day suspension – The issue has reached a wall that the employee will not be able to break through. The employee will have two days to think about how to correct the issue. Employees will either return with corrected behavior or in a destructive kamikaze haze.

4. Five-day suspension – This is the last attempt at correcting behavior and performance. This is arguably the most worthless step as your organization is most likely dealing with a problem employee who either cannot or will not change.

5. Fired – The end has come. Most organizations breathe a sigh of relief. The hiring process will begin soon to fill the vacancy.

The progressive discipline system that an organization creates must be followed consistently. There could be unforeseen obstacles creating challenges to following the steps. The author conducted a retail operation in Namibia and planned a written warning for a poor performing supervisor. Instead of humbling herself and arriving with notepad and pen in hand, she arrived with her husband. The husband appeared stern. The supervisor did not bother introducing her husband. The environment became awkward. We continued to follow our policy of explaining the poor performance while warning that the next step is suspension. It did not last that long. We mutually decided that the responsibilities of that position were greater than her capacity to serve. She left the organization and we began the hiring process soon after. As hurdles are placed in front of your progress, refer to your policy to remain on track.

Integrity

An organization must operate in integrity. As a critical component to employee retention, employer integrity includes equality, discipline, and rewards. It also includes safety and health. In the United States, unions formed partly to improve working conditions. Yet, union participation varies by both country and industry. However, integrity pushes beyond union boundaries into the culture of the organization. Without integrity companies devolve into blood sucking vampires committed only to self-preservation quantified by dollars and cents. The spirit of integrity must be present at every board meeting and considered during strategic planning. For it to be woven into the fabric of the organization, it must have the buy-in of executives who exhibit this daily.

Equality

Achieving equality appears simple; before humans get involved. Scholars and businesspersons have overintellectualizing the issue. Organizations create fancy titles such as Diversity Chief and Inclusion Director in a public attempt at reaching equality. And many of the smiling faces filling these roles wear the finest empty suits. Equality does not take graduate degrees; it requires an organization with integrity.

An organization should hire the best available candidates. This short sentence has caused emotional debate that has moonwalked on the precipice of both sexism and racism. These dividing statements will not be repeated here. The best will always rise to the top; an organization reaches equality by selecting the candidates that arrive at the top.

Equality shines its rays throughout the organization. It glides beyond the hiring process and into existing employees. A United States vehicle manufacturing company found that it had a bullying issue surrounding the race of supervisors. There were two supervisors who were ethnically different than many of their subordinates. Some of the subordinates began to harass and bully the supervisors. They hung nooses in the locker room. They wrote racial epithets on the toilet stalls. The company did not make reasonable steps to confront and stop this psychotic behavior. The supervisors quit citing threats to their security.

This organization was guilty of constructive discharge. This is a working environment made so unpleasant by the employer that the employee quits. By not creating measures to remove bullying, the organization made a silent agreement with the thugs committing the acts that their behavior was acceptable. Employers are responsible for creating an ideal workspace for all employees. This story was a homerun for the media. After national attention, and a poor financial picture, the manufacturing plant closed.

Without equality imbedded in the culture an organization can never achieve integrity. The organization will be but a vampire. A sliver of its could-have-been greatness. As a business owner or manager, it is optimal that your rise above petty insecurities that pockets of society hold against groups based on race, ethnicity, national origin, native language, age, eye and hair color, feet size, knee sturdiness, finger length or any other ridiculous prejudice surfacing. Integrity resides at the top. Stay on top.

Safety and Health

The legal boundaries pertaining to health and safety will fluctuate by jurisdiction. Integrity should have less variance. Safety and health laws are developed to ensure that employees are not required to trade their life to earn a living. Firms should support this by exceeding the limits of the law. An organization operates in integrity by ensuring employees return home as they arrived. The author served in staff for an organization that maintained high safety levels. Safety courses were conducted beyond the limits of industry standards. The best safety equipment was supplied and quickly replaced when damaged. This had a dual affect: it reduced accidents and it lowered the risk of operations.

Organizations benefit by having a healthier workforce. The benefits are numerous, and include more work output, higher morale, reduction in the cost of job injuries, and a greater reputation. That list may be arranged in ranking order by different stakeholders. Reputation should hold a special place within the hearts of every organization. Reputation is the relative to integrity. Integrity strengthens reputation and promotes a company. Wavering integrity affects the company by dampening its reputation. Organizations are not simply winning polls of public opinion. It must conduct sound operations while securing its strategic objectives. During that reach, it will find several benefits by promoting the welfare of its employees.

Conclusion

Human resources is an important area of organizational management. Do not neglect it. Taking a passive or nonchalant approach to onboarding will contribute to tremendous costs for the company. The cost of bad hires and low retention can stall or end operations. Instead, organizations must allocate necessary resources for the hiring process and team development.

The hiring process requires time from analysis to selection. The two most important phases of that process are planning and selection and it is here that organizations either contribute to the flowering spectrum of equality or expose itself as dishonest and untrustworthy. Equality is not diversity. It is not inclusion. Equality is hiring the best candidates. A separate book could be written to describe the external forces that hinder equality. During the hiring process, these forces may appear as political and familial or as race and gender prejudices.

The author held a position in an organization that fought such nepotism. The Chief Operating Officer (COO) twisted the arm of human resources into hiring her son for an administration job. His experience and education did not qualify him for the job. He was also a recently released inmate with strong ties to a large street gang. The young man was introduced in a staff meeting with the author in attendance. He could not have looked more out of place. He wore a baseball cap to disguise his ink work. Her son was covered in gang affiliated tattoos from the top of his shaven head to his fingers. For some, tattoos are no longer a taboo and the author understands that pointing out visible ink work may seem old fashioned. Got it. Now write down the number of CEOs of large companies that have tattoos on their heads and faces. Appearance matters in nearly all organizations as it, whether right or wrong, contributes to reputation.

The COO did not stop there. She demanded that her son's supervisor groom him as a successor. Her son's supervisor had over 30 years of experience and was not considering retirement. The organization, slow to render a decision, demoted the Chief Operating Officer into a middle manager position. Though the company stopped shy of dismissing her and her son, the point reverberated throughout the firm. This company does not support nepotism. Equality emerges organically from integrity.

High performance teams are the result of a successful hiring process and quality management. Management squeezes talent and abilities and serves customers a cup of synergy. The team should be challenged to achieve beyond the confines of a paradigm. Management attains high performance by holding employees accountable. Organizations that reward good behavior while disciplining poor behavior are mature and just. This also incentivizes performance while boosting morale. High performance teams do not simply appear. They are comprised of carefully selected individuals who are groomed for success. Via high performance teams, human resources make a direct and pronounced effect on operations.

74

Finance

Finance is an unavoidable subject when writing on the topic of business. I want you to find and discard two types of business books: the books that do not discuss operations and the others that do not cover finance. They are table fodder. Many great inventors, managers, and entrepreneurs fall short of their goals because of a lack of finance. It has been stated that cemeteries are rich with the ideas of the deceased. If business owners and managers are to drive their company forward, there are bottomless pits that must be avoided and creative financing ideas that must be communicated.

Within this chapter, we will discuss securing funds and company investments. First, let us remind ourselves of the below chart with operations reaching all layers. Finance will belong in the third layer. The first layer is dedicated to staff and decision making. The second to the internal culture of the organization. The third is partly dedicated to customers, suppliers, consumers, and employees. Engaging each of these third layer stakeholders will require financing.

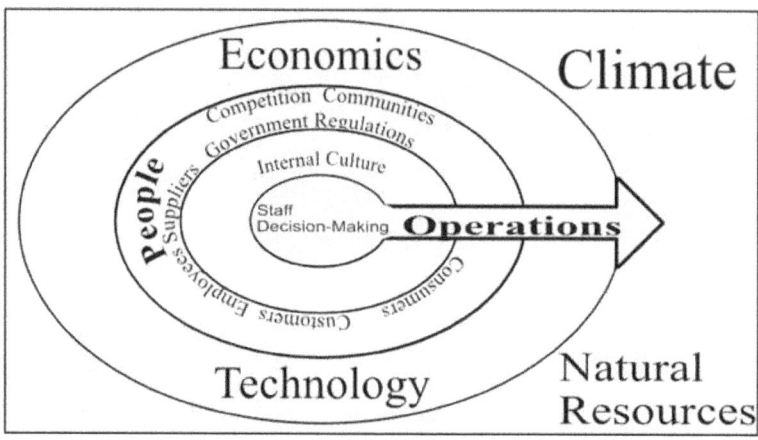

This chapter of the text will obviously contain numbers and the author is aware of the phobia that some have with digits. Get over it! By avoiding numbers and shunning accounting and finance, you either take a shot in the dark or transfer much of the important decisions of the organization to a consultant. You must understand finance to remain involved.

Additional Funds Needed

There could not be a more fitting area to begin a chapter on financing. Additional funds needed (AFN) is the decision that many organizations conclude. There is now a need for more cash than what the company current has available. This decision is reached by both large and small companies. Startups and conglomerates may see this decision alike. How the funds will be secured is where small companies and startups stand apart from larger business entities.

First, the decision to secure additional funds does not require long analysis. This conclusion is usually reached by determining that expansion is necessary. It is important to remember that greater revenue requires greater assets. For an asphalt company to stretch its area of operations from one city to three, there must be more assets. Assets will include construction equipment, perhaps a separate office for convenience, and of course more employees. Each of these assets may require additional funds.

Reaching the AFN decision is captured in an equation that most will find simple. The equation is below:

Cost of assets in growth plan – spontaneous liabilities – net profit = Additional Funds Needed

AFN in Practice

Let us walk through this. We gave a cursory view of what this asphalt company requires to expand. Now, we must approximate the value of each asset. We can hypothesize that his company will require 10 more road rollers, 10 more asphalt mixers, 20 more employees, and a new building. For easy math, we will mark these new costs at ten million dollars. The collective cost of these assets, $10,000,000, is the first figure of the above equation: cost of assets in growth plan.

The second area is spontaneous liabilities. Spontaneous liabilities are the amount in your accounts payable that your company owes for services and products that it has already received. This asphalt company purchases asphalt and receives it before paying its vendor. That is one type of spontaneous liabilities that this company has within its accounts payable. We will mark this at $100,000 and we will subtract this from the cost of assets in growth plan.

Finally, we have net profit. Of course, a company could have all the cash in its accounts to fund the growth of its operations. Businesses will still need to determine if additional funds are needed as they may consider external cash either cheaper or less risky. This asphalt company is willing to risk its net profit for this expansion. The net profit for this firm is $2,000,000. We will subtract this from the cost of assets in growth plan.

The AFN is then equal to $10,000,000 - $100,000 - $2,000,000 or $7,900,000. To expand their area of operations from one city to three cities, this company must find, at least, $7,900,000 in external cash. The fact that many startups have neither spontaneous liabilities nor net profit is not lost. In that scenario, the startup would require $10,000,000 less any personal cash in external funds. Such a startup asphalt firm would be wise to scale back from a plan of three cities to beginning with one city to reduce the cost of assets for growth.

Let us give a smaller example of a startup requiring additional funds: a barbershop. A barbershop is not as capital intensive and can have great profit margins. Perhaps equally as important, is that a grooming business is the dream of men and women throughout the planet. An entrepreneur, eyes set on a greater future, will determine the required assets and their costs. A storefront in a business residential neighborhood is best. The barber does not have plans to purchase the building; only to rent. He will need barber chairs that customers find comforting, a flat screen television for entertainment, four employees, signage on the storefront, and mirrors, hair clippers and scissors. The barber finds that the cost of these assets equal $20,000. He has worked and saved for years for this opportunity and he subtracts $5,000 in personal cash from the above $20,000. For the barber to begin operating, he will require $15,000 in additional funds.

Securing the additional funds needed is a mystery to most. It shutters businesses before they ever experience their grand openings. Many will see the $7,900,000 or $15,000 and find the task of securing that cash hopeless. That could not be further from the truth. There is money waiting to be spent on your business. As your read this book, repeatedly if necessary, you will become a more confident business owner and manager. Your strengthening abilities and towering confidence will emerge from planning. As I entered the commercial real estate industry, I had a long conversation with a business executive from a firm operating in the same space. He stated that as he and other managers planned for a large and national expansion, they received a call from an accountant representing several individuals. The individuals were from the Gulf States and they reported having over $100,000,000 to invest but could not find the right company to release the cash. This is not an exaggeration. There are investors, banks, and other organizations that would love nothing more than to invest in a quality manager with a quality plan. This is not a gift. They desperately, and openly, want to use your energy to grow their coffers.

How they enter into an agreement with your company is now what remains. Debt and equity are the two primary ways. Of course, there are other ways that we will not cover in this book. You may be willed cash from the death of a loved one. You may hit the lottery. You may have collected cans for cash on the weekend for a decade. You could write a bestselling book or sing a great song and reap the rewards of accepted intellectual property. You could use the equity from your home as a line of credit or a loan. The possibilities for securing the required cash are endless. However, we will not spend time on these other options in this text. We will look closely at both debt and equity.

Debt and Equity

Debt and equity are the two most common ways that a company raises the additional funds needed. Debt, as a capital source, consists primarily of loans from financial institutions. There are other types of debt that we will highlight as well. Companies seeking equity are offering shares of their company for cash. This can become more complicated than it appears, and we apply both education and experience in covering this decision. Risk and cost are major components of both debt and equity. For many organizations, securing capital can be either the beginning or the end of their enterprise.

Debt

Debt, at least for the purpose and simplicity of this text, consists of corporate bonds, bank loans, and investor promissory notes. The idea around debt remains consistent. The company receives cash that it is accountable for paying back with some level of interest. All three types of debt are legally binding in most nations. Generally, the decision to secure additional funds needed through debt and not equity is a decision dependent on both affordability and control. Debt allows business owners to retain the greatest control over their organization. It also puts their organization in greater risk if the company is not able to make payments. Firms choosing one debt method over another could be determined by affordability, availability, and preference.

Corporate Bond

Okay, release a corporate bond at a competitive coupon interest rate. That sentence is daunting to most business owners. The standard MBA program teaches finance, and the other business subjects, from a large multinational firm's perspective. It simply does not apply to a small or medium enterprise. As explained earlier, this is a practical text for real world application. The author will give a cursory review of releasing a corporate bond. For managers of larger companies, the information below may serve as a breakthrough. Organizations that are not yet ready to secure capital through bonds will still benefit by absorbing knowledge on these debt instruments.

Bonds are debt established as a long-term contract under which a borrower agrees to make payments of both interest and principal, on specific dates, to the holders of the bond. There are four main types of bonds, and it is important to note that cost and risk vary with each:

1. Treasury – United States Federal Government bonds are considered risk free; however, their prices decline when interest rates rise.

a. Government-sponsored entities (GSEs) include Small Business Administration (SBA), Fannie and Freddie Mac, and others. They are fully backed by the government.

2. Corporate – exposed to default risk, or credit risk. The larger the credit risk, the higher the interest rate the issuer must pay. As the business issues these corporate bonds, investors will determine the probability that the organization will default on this bond. This is important when determining the affordability of this option over others.

3. Municipal – issued by state and local governments. Exposed to default risk. No Federal tax and no state tax if you live in the same state. Munis, as these are often called, have lower interest rates than corporate bonds with the same default risk.

4. Foreign – issued by foreign governments or corporations. Both exposed to default risk. A currency risk exists if the bond is denominated in a currency other than that of the investor's home currency.

We touched on non-corporate bonds to give the reader a frame of reference. The treasury bond is an important measure of the health of an economy. The municipal and foreign bonds are great for understanding the options of your investors. Let us go further.

Bonds have specific language that may not apply in other debt and equity options. They include the par value, coupon payment, and coupon interest rate. The par value is the stated face value of the bond. It is usually $1,000; however, it can be more than this amount. The par value is simply the amount of money that the firm borrows and promises to repay when the bond matures. A maturity date represents the end of the bond agreement. A coupon payment is the fixed number of dollars of interest paid by the issuer every year, or period. This coupon payment is then divided by the par value to reach the coupon interest rate. If the par value is $1,000 and the coupon payment is $90 per year then the coupon interest rate must be 9%.

Okay, deep breath. The student has an obligation to learn and the teacher has an obligation not to bore. Bonds can become very detailed and specific. We will not dig that deep. That is not within the scope of this text. We are simply providing a cursory coverage of bonds.

The reason that corporate bonds are not an option for most small companies is the event risk associated with such an investment. This is the chance that an event will occur and increase the credit risk of a company, hence lowering the firm's bond rating and the value of its outstanding bonds; companies with this risk looming, must pay higher interest rates. If availability and affordability are the two main factors for organizations securing capital, the risk associated with a young company with limited assets may render this option unaffordable.

Bond ratings are based on both quantitative and qualitative factors, such as the organization's financial ratios, bond contract terms, and the quality of its labor. The above list is an overview of how bond ratings are reached. The bond rating is correlated with both risk and affordability. A bond's rating is an indicator of its default risk; and therefore, the rating has a direct and measurable influence on the bond's yield. Higher risk equates to a higher expected reward for investors and higher cost for organizations issuing bonds.

Bank Loans

Like bonds above and promissory notes below, bank loans are a liability. The organization must pay the loan back, on schedule, or find itself on the wrong side of a courtroom. Bank loans may seem like an unsurmountable task for a company with few assets to secure the debt. Organizations securing capital, could use both equity and debt. First, it can help in reaching the down payment threshold. Second, it will also reduce the default risk that is attributed to a company that may not be able to pay its debt on schedule. Bank loans can satisfy many capital requirements.

Bank loans, and other debt as well, keep managers within clear boundaries. Organizations that secure debt to finance their growth will be careful to not default on the loan. This allows them to potentially be more mindful managers. Managers will usually reduce expenses by looking through the company with a critical eye. It may also slow the company down as risky behaviors will be shunned for a safer option. Riskier decisions have greater rewards.

CR Patterson & Sons. Yet, even with this careful management, events in the external environment may still arrive at the organization's door. A great example of this is CR Patterson & Sons, a company that changed its product lines to adapt to a changing transportation environment. The company began in the 19th century with founder Charles Richard Patterson creating surreys. These surreys were the norm in family transportation throughout the United States of America. However, there was disruptive innovation on the horizon: the automobile.

The company adapted by creating the Patterson-Greenfield automobile. It was a great craft of vehicle art. It was handmade and it was affordable. The first external hurdle that the company was forced to handle was the Detroit competitors that could produce at a greater capacity because of assembly lines. CR Patterson & Sons, now into its second generation, adapted successfully to competition by becoming a supplier of auto bodies. Led by Frederick Douglas Patterson, the founder's son, the company earned greater profits. All seemed well until the Great Depression staggered the economy.

The external environment battered CR Patterson & Sons. The Great Depression would last from 1929 – 1939. Frederick's sons were not able to see the light at the end of the tunnel. After multiple generations in business, the company switched off their lights for the final time in 1939. All companies must control its internal environment while keeping an eye on external factors. A company with debt will have less space and time to adjust to these changes and could find its business closed quicker.

Investor Promissory Note

The promissory note is a common method for securing debt outside of a banking institution. They are more negotiable, and more power is shifted to the company issuing the debt than a bank loan. You set the terms of the note. The debtor can establish the length of the promissory note, the interest owed to the lender, and the how and when a lender receives payment. A note could have the following terms:

Five-year promissory note with an annual 10% simple interest paid on or before December 21st.

If a lender invested $100,000 under this note, the organization would be required to pay $10,000 each of the first four years and $110,000 during the fifth and final year. The grand total due to the investor is $150,000. It would be a mistake to sign this document and think that payment is optional. Promissory notes are debt and they are treated as such in most courts of law.

Capital Structure

Naturally, many young and seasoned managers will wonder how much debt they should acquire. More will wonder if they should give equity to investors. This balance is called capital structure and these questions should find answers internally while considering industry standards. In the technology field, debt is a much lower percentage of raised capital. For utilities companies, the debt to equity ratio is higher; yet, debt remains a fraction of equity. Research and preference are key here. A company with only one option for raising capital has an easy choice. As the business establishes sales, managers will create the ideal debt to equity picture to propel the organization.

For companies with revenue, business orthodoxy prescribes a pecking order for raising capital. In this pecking order, a company reinvests its net income to fund assets used for growth. The second step in the pecking order is to issue debt in the form of bonds or investor promissory notes for smaller firms. Equity is given only when net income and debt does not cover the required cash. Again, this is business orthodoxy and it examines raising capital from an uncreative angle. At times, organizations may rather issue equity to gain the experience and knowledge of the investor. A strategic investor may have established business inroads that can result in further contracts. An organization must raise capital based on affordability, availability, and preference.

Equity

Equity is the other side of the capital coin. As explained above, capital structure cannot be simplified into an elementary decision on whether to give equity to an investor or place debt within the organization. Often, organizations look to find balance in raising the additional funds needed. Business schools spend large amount of time teaching the value of the initial public offering (IPO). Companies may also find that raising capital with an accredited investor or a trusting friend is more organic and better fits their situation. We will cover these three options with the understanding that equity in the 21st century is complicated and can expand beyond this boundary.

Initial Public Offering (IPO)

The IPO is the most explained and championed method for raising capital in most business schools. Business professors explain the beauty and pitfalls of this primary market without much thought that many young businesses are not close to this stage of maturity. Of course, the curriculum at most accredited business schools are formed to generate the best middle and executive managers at established for profit companies. For some firms, the IPO is important for raising additional funds needed. Therefore, we will cover it as a tool in finance.

The IPO is out of reach for most companies, not because their managers do not possess the knowhow, but rather because of the costs associated with this option. Business education leans strongly to quantitative decisions. Decisions are based on numbers and those numbers are verified continuously. If this theory holds, then the IPO is simply too expensive for most companies. There are costs associated with the investment bank, lawyers, accountants, underwriter, and printers. These are costs that most startups and small companies cannot bear.

Once the plan to release shares is announced, the organization sends a team on a road show to secure institutional investors. This is another cost for a small or medium enterprise. The more managers that an organization has working on securing capital, the least you have performing operations. For larger companies, this process may slow operations; yet, for small companies it may contribute to defaulting on an existing contract.

The IPO is released from the company and institutional investors purchase the shares before the offering is available to the general public through the stock market. If the value is reasonable, this is a great way for companies to secure cash. Post IPO daily trading on the stock market represents the secondary market and the company does not directly profit from that trade. An initial public offering is staunchly regulated in most nations and this vehicle stands juxtaposed to the next two equity options.

Accredited Investor

Finding an accredited investor is simple, finding an accredited investor that will invest in your business takes work. This text provides the reader with the managerial knowledge to secure accredited investors by talking their language and unveiling a reasonable and attainable plan. This text does not simply provide the suit, but it also offers the brains. Accredited investors are measuring the capacity of the chief executive as much as the figures on the cash flow projections. Similarly, business owners should investigate the investor.

The author, while doing business in Botswana for several years, met an accredited investor that seemed to be the ideal partner. We were building an accommodation facility and he had several. We toured his hotels and safari lodges in a neighboring country prior to our business meeting. He was peaked at the idea of entering our area of operation and most importantly, his team and mine all seemed to click. Things felt good as we left the meeting and returned to our hotel. The next day, we flew home. For the next couple of weeks, the author spoke to the investor over the phone. The conversation was no longer about if he should invest but rather a negotiation over ownership shares. We reached an agreement. Excited, I hurried the news to my team. That afternoon, we celebrated and that night we sat in charrette, light on words, calculating our next steps.

Our accredited investor was no longer in the picture. The deal was off. There was no individual or company to blame. We had simply not completed our due diligence on the investors qualifications to invest with a company or person from the United States. This individual was, and still is at the writing of this text (2020), on the Specially Designated National (SDN) list. You never heard of it, right? No worries, you are not alone. The SDN list is compiled by the United States Treasury and the list includes individuals sanctioned by the US Government for various crimes and allegations. United States Citizens are prohibited from conducting business with such Specially Designated Nationals.

There we were, a team with a project well within its second phase without the capital to complete the project. Our lawyer chirped resource-draining ideas of petitioning the United States Government to excuse this one person from a sanctions list. Others wanted to discuss workarounds. Many sat in silent disappointment. I cheered them up by absorbing the blame. If anyone was to blame, it was us. We should have done our research. We should have forwarded the investor's name by the United States Embassy for their approval. There were several boxes left unchecked that could have stopped the conversation long before an agreement. Yet, we learned. We learned to never let cash place a veil over the process. Our team dusted the disappointment off and secured the additional, and legal, capital to move forward.

Family and Friends

Accredited investors have a high net worth. Many family and friends do not. However, they know your skills and abilities. They have seen you work in that field for years and heard your plans for months. They may not have $100,000 to give at once. Yet, collectively, they are a great option for small and medium needs. The barber, explained earlier in the text, may find that raising the necessary $15,000 is quicker than debt. Few accredited investors will consider a $15,000 investment as the return is too low.

Entrepreneurs should avoid taking advantage of family and friends because of their proximity and agreeableness. It is still advisable to have a plan and share it with whoever expresses interest. There will be some family members who will practically throw cash toward the business idea. This can be a trap for startups! Easy cash given by careless investors can make the business owner complacent and push aside proper planning to lunge deeper into operations. The plans are not simply to lure an investor. Plans are necessary to drive operations and develop a stronger management team. For the relaxed investor, entrepreneurs should take steps to read the most important summaries within your plans. This way, the investor will understand that they are not simply a dollar sign and that the company has every intention of making this transaction a rewarding one.

Whatever It Takes

The above section on raising additional funds needed will mean different things to different business owners. Entrepreneurs should read the above text and begin to have ideas on how they will secure the capital required to convert their plans into operations. Whether debt or equity, a plan must be initiated with a 'whatever it takes' thesis. The author, having started a storefront in Namibia knows about whatever it takes.

The resolve and determination to start a company in a foreign land is nearly unmatched. When we created a beauty store in Namibia, my wife and I were foreigners. We did not have an established relationship with a local bank to secure a loan or a line of credit. We were simply foreign direct investors, isolated from our base. It is a courageous decision for any young businessperson to take. In additional to courage, the decision is also filled with risks.

Establishing consistent cash flow should be a major focus of any company. We planned the renovations with built-in shelving, signage, large inventory sourced from multiple companies, and a sizable staff. We knew what we wanted, but not precisely how to squeeze it in on our budget. The decision was quickly reached to live in the shop. We planned out a section of the large store, added materials to our renovation costs, constructed a room in the back with warm lights and bedding, and began to sleep in our shop. Our customers did not catch on and we rested well knowing that we saved on living expenses. It was also a great way to become totally submerged in the business.

Eula McClaney

Eula McClaney is another, grander, story of whatever it takes. Eula was born in a semi-slavery system called Jim Crow in the American South. As part of a family engaged in the cotton industry, she saw how the debt system of Jim Crow kept individuals enslaved. She, and her husband, found a way to break from that vicious and racist cycle to find better living in the North. She had a vision that if she planned, things would fall in place. Eula planned, prayed, and worked. Hard. She cleaned homes. She sold baked goods. She babysat. She did whatever it took to bring the family more cash while her husband worked in the steel mill. She purchased her first property, and then another, and another. Before long, she owned dozens of properties. She moved West and used her grit, experience, knowledge, and perseverance to duplicate her past success. Eula became a self-made multimillionaire against seemingly insurmountable odds.

It is important for the reader to understand that whatever odds you face, whatever hardships and rocky mountainsides are before you, that someone has made it from the same position. The gritty win. The man that knows he has something to offer will not sit on a curb the first time the bank says no. The woman that can envision the path to success should not kick rocks if the accredited investor is not interested. Keep pushing to finance your operations. Scale back, if necessary, to propel your company into the industry. Learn. Be flexible. Be persistent.

Financial Statements and Plans

There are several financial statements and plans that managers must learn and develop. Most business schools focus on three statements: balance sheet, cash flow, and income. This could be considered the primary group. This text will add another two plans that are vital to understanding the full financial picture: breakeven analysis and personnel plan. The reader is encouraged to find additional plans that work with their organization and industry.

For startups, many of the statements will be projections. Projections are researched based guesses that are usually too optimistic. Projections should be compared to industry averages and reformed with greater accuracy as the planning horizon nears. Many entrepreneurs have mixed emotions as they make the leap. Many managers experience confidence highs and lows as they climb the corporate ladder. Most of the entrepreneurs and managers will have an outward shell of optimism that they share with the world. If you see them in the grocery store, they may rattle off a strategic objective. If you find them in a cafeteria, they may tell you the total sales in their industry and how much their company would be worth if they only secured 1% of that. They will go on and on over a phone about their budding idea. All of this is optimism and much of it is a mask. Optimism is great when it does not conceal reality. Projections should be realistic and must not assume a piece of the market share pie.

Balance Sheet

A balance sheet positions assets against liabilities and owner's equity. This can be simple for startups and complex for operating companies. For startups, the standard is usually to project your assets before you begin operations. For established companies, the balance sheet will be an accurate snapshot. It is important that the balance sheet is completed by the company's managers, especially in the organization's infancy.

Kasane Asphalt Balance Sheet
In thousands

Assets		Liabilities	
Current Assets		**Current Liabilities**	
Cash	20	Accounts Payable	120
Inventory	200		
Accounts Receivable	250		
Total Current Asset	**470**	**Total Current Liabilites**	**120**
Plant and Equipment	600	Long-Term Debt	500
Total Assets	**1070**	**Total Liabilities**	**620**
		Retained Earnings	450
		Total Liabilities and Retained Earnings	**1070**

Current assets are separated from the asset category to categorize assets that not only *can* convert to cash but probably *will* be converted in the next 12 months. Cash, inventory, and accounts receivables all fall within this category. Current assets are significant as they signify that an organization can pay its liabilities. In the above example, Kasane Asphalt has $470,000 in current assets.

Plant and Equipment can be expanded to show greater detail. It includes land, buildings, and other immovable assets. It also includes the equipment necessary for operations. In the case of this fictious company, Kasane Asphalt will have rollers and earth moving machines.

Current liabilities are also separated from long-term liabilities to show the immediate liability concerns. Of course, all liabilities can tank a company, so all of them are important. However, these accounts payable represent cash that are immediately owed to other organizations. A company that has greater current liabilities than current assets could be in trouble, or it could be a startup. In the above example, Kasane Asphalt is in a good position as assets are greater than liabilities. This is captured by positive retained earnings.

If completed correctly, total assets will equal total liabilities and retained earnings. There is no magic trick to getting it right. If you arrive at two separate numbers, find where the digit was misplaced and correct. The balance sheet is a dynamic financial statement that must be updated frequently to communicate an accurate message on the health of the company.

Income Statement

An income statement, or profit and loss statement, is a common and important financial statement. It will be a requirement of banks and intelligent investors alike. Like the balance sheet above, the income statement can include several line items. The income statement below takes an elementary approach to instruction with the idea that the reader and business manager will expand and adjust accordingly.

If the business has yet to conduct operations, then it must create a projected income statement. The below example will still apply. The difference is that the manager who prepares the projected income statement will use industry-based research and organizational plans to complete the statement and not actual data from the previous year.

Niani Data Center Income Statement	
	In thousands
Sales	2000
Cost of Goods Sold	700
Marketing	250
Payroll	400
Utilities	60
Insurance	20
Earnings before interest and taxes (EBIT)	570
Interest Cost	200
Earnings before taxes (EBT) or Pre-tax Earnings	370
Taxes	93
Net Profit (or loss)	278

In the above income statement example, Niani Data Center has two million dollars in sales. This is great. Not simply great because of its size but also very good because of the possibility for growth in a sustainable industry. Data Centers are springing up throughout the world as data storage and retrieval seeps their way into the culture of organizations within various industries.

The cost of goods sold can also be the cost of services sold. These are the inputs that allow the sale to happen. For a data center, these are the large computers necessary to store data. For a bakery, the cost of goods sold will include flour, sugar, and eggs. For Kasane Asphalt, the cost of goods will include heavy equipment, cement, and asphalt. The cost of goods sold is a great line item that should be expanded and broke down to display the full detail. This is a great area for future cost savings.

The cost for marketing is nearly always justified. Usually, it is the line item that could use more cash. Allocating money into marketing is money well spent as it increases contracts and sales. Your target market must know your business exists.

The author was hired as a consultant for a manufacturing company. The company produces great products in the energy sector. They had a decent, though a bit stale, management staff. On paper, the executives were qualified to be at the helm. They seemed to create consistent and dependable products. Yet, there was a major issue in the company. Very few people had ever heard of them! Their website was old and outdated. They refused to use social media to get their product some brand awareness. They were captives to unproductive thinking.

The solution seemed simple, until their board blocked my marketing budget. It was clear, for the moment, that the executives wanted more sales but did not want to pay for it. We reached a comfortable medium: the organization agreed to hire an external marketing company that specialized in search engine optimization and social media presence. Their sales increased beyond the additional cost of marketing. A smart company is willing to spend cash on marketing to increase revenue.

It is not uncommon for payroll to be the greatest expense for a company. In the above example, it is the second largest cost the organization must bear. As seen in the human resources chapter, employees are a great resource for a company and their pay deserves careful consideration. Startups may struggle to retain key talent without a competitive compensation plan. For seasoned companies, there are usually no viable excuses for poorly compensating employees.

Utilities and Insurance are expenses that an organization will not be able to escape. Utilities will fluctuate based on the size and nature of the business. Insurance is often dependent on the type of operations. A construction firm will require specific insurance to transfer risk. The mistake comes when small companies *forget* to include insurance. The barbershop and the nail technician also require insurance to cover their assets and livelihoods in case of an accident. It is imperative that small businesses remember insurance.

The next figure we see is earnings before interest and taxes. This is equal to sales minus expenses. For Niani Data Center, this figure stands at $570,000. This is an important number for businesses as it shows the health of the company before mandatory payments of tax and interest.

Interest is for debt repayment. Once this is subtracted from the above equation, the organization is left with the earnings before taxes. Taxes fluctuate by region and in this example, we used a 25% tax rate. We are left with a net profit. If the company was not profitable during this period, we will find a net loss.

Statement of Cash Flows

Cash flow is vital to operations. Cash flow, more so than immediate profitability, shows that the company has growth potential. Specifically, a company that has good cash flow exhibits the ability to purchase the assets required to grow. Besides additional funds required to grow, the statement of cash flows is used to determine if a firm can pay its liabilities. For startup companies, business owners and managers will create the cash flow projection. It is a required statement for both investors and banks. It is common for those parties to demand a 12-month or even a 36-month statement. This statement does not require divination. Follow the steps below, use industrial research, and make professional estimates.

Atlantic Grocer
Statement of Cash Flows

	in thousands
Operating Activities	
Net Income	3000
Increase in accounts receivables	-400
Increase in inventories	-1400
Increase in accounts payable	50
Net Cash provided (used) by operating activities	**1250**
Investing Activities	
Cash to purchase fixed assets	-1000
Proceeds from sale of property	100
Net cash provided (used) by investing activities	**-900**
Financing Activities	
Borrowings of long-term debt	500
Debt interest payments	-50
Net Cash provided (used) by financing activities	**450**
Summary	
Net change in cash	800
Cash at the beginning of the year	250
Cash at the end of the year	**1050**

In this example, Atlantic Grocer is an operating supermarket. The statement of cash flows is prepared for the previous annual period. Many banks and investors will demand to see cash flows broken down to months. This will allow trends and cash flow fluctuations to be easily apparent. The preparations are the same, only broken down by monthly records.

Net income for Atlantic Grocer is three million. This may seem impressive to the untrained eye. However, an understanding of the fast-moving consumer goods industry reveals that this company is a very small organization.

Accounts receivables and inventory are both current assets. Any increase in current assets will decrease cash. This is a positive action; the company is not stagnant in operating activities. Finally, an increase in accounts payable, a current liability, increases cash. We sum the figures to reach the net cash provided by operating activities.

The next category for the statement of cash flows is the investing activities. For operating companies, a big decrease in cash to purchase fixed assets means growth. This is a great sign the company has a management staff focused on the planning horizon and not bogged down with short-sighted decisions. If there are any fixed assets or short-term investments sold, it will clearly be itemized as an increase in cash. For organizations determined to grow, net cash provided by investing activities will usually be negative.

Financing activities include raising capital for operations. When organizations borrow from banks, it is written as notes payable. For other debt instruments, it is often written as borrowings of long-term debt. For Atlantic Grocer, $500,000 entered their organization, increasing cash, by an accredited investor. The interest on that debt is 10% annual, and the statement of cash flows reflects this agreement.

The summary first adds together each category. For this fictious company, the net change in cash is $800,000. There are not necessarily right or wrong answers here. The results will fluctuate based on where the company is in its maturity cycle. A young budding startup may have a negative net change in cash for years. For an established company, a negative net change in cash will certainly cause alarm.

The cash at the beginning of the year is added to the above amount to reach the cash at the end of the year. For Atlantic Grocer, the company has $1,050,000 in cash.

Every manager should be familiar with each of the three financial statements. The balance sheet, income statement, and statement of cash flows are the foundation for communicating an organization's financial situation. The statements share information and that integration will usually result in a correct or incorrect preparation for the bundle.

Additional Financial Planning

Of course, there is more to financial communication beyond the above financial statements. This text will focus on two financial plans: the breakeven analysis and the personnel plan.

Breakeven Analysis

The breakeven analysis is a very important tool for not only startups but established companies injecting cash into the business. It is used to form good business decisions. Dauman Technologies, a fictitious company, created a breakeven analysis. While the three main financial statements can either be an accurate picture or a projection, the breakeven analysis always projects into the future. Often, the analysis considers five years after the investment. However, if the breakeven point is further in the future, then the analysis must be extended.

Dauman Technologies Breakeven Analysis

	Year 1	Year 2	Year 3	Year 4	Year 5
Initial Capital	300,000.00	-	-	-	-
Revenue	400,000.00	448,000.00	501,760.00	561,971.20	629,407.74
Expenses	240,000.00	268,800.00	301,056.00	337,182.70	377,644.65
Earnings Before Interest and Taxes (EBIT)	160,000.00	179,200.00	200,704.00	224,788.50	251,763.10
Earnings Before Taxes (EBT) {22%}	130,000.00	149,200.00	170,704.00	194,788.50	221,763.10
Net Profit	101,400.00	116,376.00	133,149.12	151,935.03	172,975.22
Retained Earnings	-198,600.00	-82,224.00	50,925.12	202,860.15	375,835.37

The Break-Even Point (Return on Investment) is projected within the second (2nd) 52 week year starting from the first week of operation.

The business owner has researched the industry that he intends to enter and placed the initial capital at a reasonable $300,000. This breakeven analysis considers the next five years of his company. He places the revenue of his company at $400,000. For the next years, he projects a 12% growth in annual revenue. Therefore, by year five, he projects revenue of $629,407.74. Expenses are captured at $240,000 during year one. The business owner places expenses as 60% of revenue. He will keep this as a generic standard until he begins operations and has more accurate accounting.

He reaches Earnings Before Interest and Taxes (EBIT). This is simply revenue minus expenses (400,000 − 240,000 = 160,000). Interest will remain at 10% throughout the life of the loan. This interest payment amounts to $30,000 (300,000 * 10%). Next is Earnings Before Taxes (EBT). This is the arithmetic equation of subtracting interest payment from EBIT (160,000 − 30,000) to reach $130,000. For this example, we are setting the tax rate at 22%. The net profit is $101,400 for the first year of operation.

For the breakeven analysis, it is the retained earnings that we are most concerned. For the first year, the company has not yet broken even on its initial capital. In fact, the company will not breakeven until the third year. For investors and business owners, this should be considered reasonable. There are several organizations that required nearly a decade to breakeven and drew investors during that building period. Therefore, the breakeven analysis is a tool to adjust expectations and should be used, with other tools, to make sound business decisions.

The above is not to pretend that there are not breakeven red flags. A company that does not have a proprietary upside in a relatively flat industry should breakeven soon. A company, such as a barbershop, that breaks even in six years is in trouble. Either the expenses are too high, or it is in the wrong area and will suffer from depressing revenue.

With the above example for Dauman Technologies, it operates in a technology field that is swiftly changing. That brings risk to the stability of a five-year revenue projection. However, if we assume that it has proprietary products and great staff then we can suggest that it will foresee and stay ahead of the tide of change. For startups, the most stable lines in a breakeven analysis are the initial capital and interest payment. The other lines are subject to change; and change dramatically.

Personnel Plan

The personal plan is a very important tool that should be created before the income statement. Payroll is covered in the income statement; however, the organization needs details to move forward with confidence. This personnel plan is especially important for startups. Though many investors and banks will not require the plan, it should be created for internal reference.

King Motel Personnel Plan

	Year 1
General and Primary Manager @ 6,000 Monthly	72,000.00
Sales and Marketing Manager @ 5,000 Monthly	60,000.00
Food and Beverage Manager @ 5,000 Monthly	60,000.00
2 Receptionists @ 3,500 each, Monthly	84,000.00
3 Housekeepers @ 2,500 each, Monthly	90,000.00
2 Cooks @ 3,000 each, Monthly	72,000.00
3 Waiters/Waitresses @ 2,500 each, Monthly	90,000.00
2 Maintenance Employees @ 4,500 each, Monthly	108,000.00
2 Security Guards @ 3,000 each, Monthly	72,000.00
Total Payroll	**708,000.00**
Payroll Burden @ 20%	**141,600.00**
Total Payroll Expenditures	**849,600.00**

In this example, an entrepreneur purchased an existing motel. She has completed her due diligence, secured the capital required to purchase the building, and has completed the business plan with financials. To create the above personnel plan, she used the operational records of the seller and additional industry research.

There are less descriptive ways to create the personnel plan. You may choose to hide both the number of employees per position and the amount paid. Instead, you can place it in the text below the plan. It may also be preferred to create a monthly personnel loan instead of annual. A personnel plan showing the cost per month is especially useful in seasonal businesses. A landscaping company in Chicago should use a more descriptive monthly personnel plan to capture spikes of employment in the spring and summer months.

For King Motel, the total payroll for the 17 employees is $708,000. The payroll burden is often ignored. This burden is dependent on external governmental factors such as retirement contribution and health care. We put the burden at 20% for this motel. This is an important factor to consider and plan for; ignoring it can in turn either hurt your financial picture or open your organization up to liability. The total payroll expenditures represent the number that King Motel must plan for: $849,600. Without the personnel plan, the stated cost for payroll is nothing more than a murky guess.

Budget

The budget of a company is a forward plan that usually considers the next 12 to 60 months. A budget may appear like a summary of assets that the company will purchase. Yet, to reach that summary of assets managers must analyze projects to find the best path forward for the organization. Projects, here, are the basis for increasing assets.

Projects and Assets

The analysis of a potential project can either be cursory or detailed. The nature and flow of projects are covered more carefully and in fuller detail in the Operations chapter. In this chapter we cover project selection in connection with the budget. The idea that projects should be selected for any reason other than a financial one is a muted point throughout business orthodoxy. However, they do occur.

Sacred cows are projects that are unresearched but pushed from the top as an important direction for the organization. For small companies, sacred cows are more dangerous. This danger is not simply because a smaller firm has less margin for error; but, also because of the greater probability and frequency for untrained management. We can paint the picture of a technician, in a room with her husband, deciding to go after the project that they dreamed about for years. This occurs often in young companies as technicians operate business like a fantasy. In this environment, full planning is often overlooked and ignored.

A sacred cow, unplanned and forced, can end a company faster than it started. Quality managers will push for an analysis of projects to find the most financially beneficial option. Before managers spend time with quantitative analysis, they must answer a broad qualitative question to determine qualification. They must determine if this 'thing' they are considering is even a project at all.

A project is a temporary endeavor to achieve a unique result, product, or service. The temporary nature of a project is highlighted with a proposed start and end date. Naturally, the reader may wonder if the project is temporary then why does the life of the assets supporting the project outlast the project itself. Projects can establish operations. The assets secured for the project are either used for a separate project later or absorbed in daily operations.

If the 'thing' considered is indeed a project, the manager must continue into qualitative analysis. There are three primary quantitative analyses that an organization must perform: net present value, internal rate of return, and breakeven analysis. We have explained the breakeven analysis and will not cover it again here. Both Net present value (NPV) and internal rate of return (IRR) calculation are beyond the scope of this book. The author does encourage business owners and managers to purchase a financial calculator and take the time to learn these two important calculations.

Net present value, though not thoroughly explained in this book, discounts future cash flows to determine the financial value of the project. NPV is a great gatekeeper that gives an awesome financial picture on a potential project. Internal rate of return is a great measure for comparing the cost of capital with expected returns. If the IRR is greater than the cost of capital, then the organization has a viable project. If the cost is less than the cost of capital, then the organization is projected to bleed money.

Conclusion

Finance is a necessity for nearly all varieties of companies. Organizations become creative in securing cash. They reach out to investors, family members, and approach bankers. All of the above is completed with the stated goal of getting a business off the ground or leaping into a project that they foresee as profitable. Wherever you find successful entrepreneurs, you will find the drive to succeed. There is an exuding energy that this thing, this organization, is more than possible; it is probable. Often, it starts with a dream or a goal, but it nearly always passes through the planning phase of finance.

Many plans have failed the quality test and companies paid the price for this shortcoming. Many companies are teetering by the wayside because it was convenient to jump into the sea of business without planning for finance. When managers plan for external cash, they must allocate considerable time to ensuring that their idea is profitable. They must research their industry and provide a realistic idea of their companies standing in that market. Financial statements are great tools for communicating the current health and horizon of a company. These living documents are dynamic with figures changing with the organization's evolving reality.

The capital structure is also dynamic. An organization faced with investor rejection may finance an overwhelming majority of assets with debt. As the company ages, it will reduce the debt. The company, when approaching a new project, may have greater options for equity capital. There is an average capital structure for each industry. Managers research this average, while understanding their own constraints, and form the best balance to move the organization forward. Debt is riskier than equity, but it is that riskiness that keeps managers disciplined. Balance is certainly imperative in capital structure.

Once operating, managers select projects that grow the organization financially. These projects are compared with each other in competition for limited resources. Once a decision is reached, the company will secure any additional funds required to ensure that project's success. Finance does not halt at this point. Managers continually strive to keep the company in good financial standing. Once the cash is flowing into the organization, much of it should be reinvested. This is particularly important for small companies. Reinvesting means that the company either uses the cash directly for projects or puts it in low risk investments. Low risk investments include bonds and real estate. A business owner, with an eye on diversity, can exhibit creativity in setting the organization's portfolio. Whichever decision is made is superior to purchasing more cars and homes for family and friends. For a small company, such behavior is merely fleecing the company of its future. Financial discipline is a virtue for managers.

Operations

The preceding chapters were a preface to Operations. The author stresses an operations focused organization throughout this text. Operations is not a step; it is the engine of your organization. It is distinct in its similarities and expansive in its differences between industries. Professors have faced consistent criticism that too few among them have real world experience. Many students at the bachelors and masters level prefer professors with operational experience prior to their tenure. It brings the course to life. Many business subject authors also have either a linear career or no experience. The author shares his ideas to success not simply attained from having earned a Master of Business Administration (MBA) or multiple designations in project management and information technology; but also, through global experience.

The author has worked in five countries for over a year each. Besides USA, these countries are in Southern Africa and Asia. Tasks included everything from establishing a project management office to filing papers. The author has entrepreneurial experience managing diverse teams that spoke English as a foreign language and worked in subordination to brilliant managers and professionals. Industries include construction, public utilities, real estate, armed forces, and retail.

We have arrived back at our favorite chart.

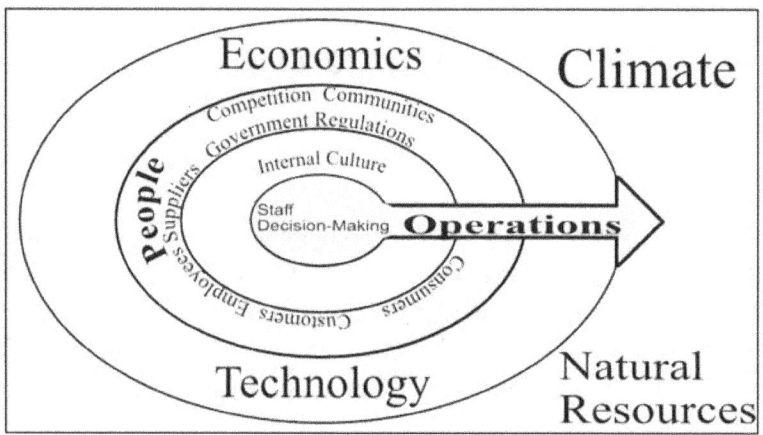

Operations touches each element of the organization. It touches the staff and should be the primary focus of business decisions. In the Finance chapter, we spoke briefly on sacred cows and their negative waywardness. As executives push sacred cows down steam, the cause is often loss as employees scramble to get the project complete. The primary cause of sacred cows is executives losing focus of operations. Once operations are no longer the focus, each manager will come to the table with an agenda. That agenda may be personal fame. That agenda may be a rising share price at all costs. That agenda may be to return a favor. We have seen each of these agendas lead to corruption, a foundering company, and more negative ripples affecting society at large.

Operations will affect culture. Companies operating in the software technology space are usually more relaxed than law firms. This leads to the next sphere: People. Operations will determine who are your customers and suppliers. It will also determine what laws and regulations apply to your business concern. Operations pushes further into technology. Technology and the economy are the next sphere that impact markets differently. Operations must consider these as well as elements that our not in management's control: natural resources and our climate.

In this text, we will provide insight in strategic alignment, policies and procedures, learning cultures, and procurement. This chapter will also explain the benefits of information technology and professional project management. In addition to explaining benefits, this text points the reader into useful application of operations. This chapter, and book, is for both the seasoned operations manager with 30 years of experience and the neophyte who needs help walking through basic project management. This text is neither to belittle the high school dropout nor congratulate the men and women with special letters behind their name. The great motivational speaker, Les Brown, once told an audience that he also earned an MBA. The group of executives, who paid to hear Les speak and knew of his educational background, looked puzzled. They knew that Les only had a high school education. The audience erupted with laughter as Les Brown cleared up his comment, stating that 'My MBA is a Major Bank Account!' This text is for one and all who desire to be a more well-rounded manager and business owner.

Strategic Alignment

Strategic alignment places the focus of operations on the established and current strategy of the company. An organization that operates outside of its strategy has lost focus and will lose energy. Energy equates to cash, time, and morale. The cash will seep out when unnecessary assets are purchased. The time spent by staff and employees to make a visionless project come to life can never be reused. The morale of employees, often ignored by staff, will wane as buy-in disappears. Buy-in puts verve into operations. It allows employees to work diligently with a genuine belief that their efforts have a meaningful contribution. A company without the buy-in of employees will find employees robotically moving from task to task. These employees either do not believe in the vision of the organization or do not believe they contribute to achieving that vision. Strategic alignment is a focus of executive management.

Aligning operations of a company to its planned strategy is achieved through three primary actions: communication and education, goals for individuals, and rewards for performance. A lack of these factors can create a revolving door where employees look for a better employer within the first year of their hire. Positively, these factors can also create an environment where success is the norm and employees enjoy their workspace.

Communication and Education

Implementing a strategy requires educating through communicating to those the organization will look to execute that strategy. This will include not only internal stakeholders, such as employees; but also, external stakeholders, such as vendors and local government. Employees and staff, in exchange for appropriate communication on operations will provide buy-in. This buy-in is not static. It can change and must be managed. Communicating and educating employees of the direction of the company is but a single factor for buy-in. Other factors include job safety, job security, promotions, raises, and personal issues. Communication should be planned and formal.

Communication, which includes educating on the elements of the operations, should not be an informal meeting in the cafeteria. There is a time for filling in details in the hallways of the office. Yet, the foundation of strategic alignment is purposeful and planned. The audience should include the entire roster of the organization. Because of shifts and the need to keep operations undisturbed, there may be many small speeches by management.

For established companies, this is an opportunity to show the highlights of the previous year or period. Highlights should explain how tasks contributed to achieving the strategic vision. The budget should be shared and compared to actual results. This is not a time for smearing the numbers. Be open and honest. If you missed your target for sales in the 4th quarter, give a good explanation on the shortcoming and set another goal for the coming year. For startup organizations, managers have an equally important task ahead of them. They must communicate expectations and show with confidence how it aligns with the strategic visions and projections.

External stakeholders also require communication and education. What the organization shares with vendors and other external stakeholders will certainly be limited. Companies should only share noncompetitively sensitive information with these stakeholders. The budget and performance variance should certainly be kept internal. Vacancies on key positions should be communicated. An idea of how the vendor will best serve within the strategic vision of the organization should also be covered.

There are other types of communication that are important in organizations. These are more informal and allow the audience to read at their leisure. These communications include memos and newsletters. The mode of communication is usually email and they consist of operationally important content. There are further informal one on one talks that help drive home a point to a specific employee or vendor manager. These talks, or personal emails, should clearly state the expectations that the manager holds for the recipient. Personal communications to key individuals may prove more effective than a formal speech in boosting performance.

Goals for Individual Performance - STRAFOG

Strategy must be drilled down into goals for individuals to accomplish. We have seen and heard the acronym SMART to describe Specific, Measurable, Attainable, Relevant, and Time-Based goals. This acronym is demanded throughout organizational departments and divisions. Though it has received a lot of attention within the past decade, supervisors still fail in having this align with strategy.

Creating goals for individual employees usually comes at the beginning of the calendar year and is an important moment for both the employee and the employer. These goals are written agreements on expectations that the employees are to answer for at the end of the year. In some organizations, these goals are printed and signed by employee and supervisors. Other companies correlate rewards, such as bonuses, to performance of stated goals. These goals are written as statements. These statements should contain goals that are specific, measurable, attainable, relevant, and time-based. This directive produces subpar goals for two reasons: strong judgment free relationships and confusion.

The author was a leading member of a multi-divisional steering committee formed to boost productivity. The data was evident, regardless of task, performance varied widely. However, there were few disciplinary actions to punish the poor behavior. We ordered the SMART goals of the employees; hundreds of them. After scouring the papers, it became clear that the employees with the longest tenure at the organization, and thus the strongest relationships, had the most ambiguous and soft goals. While the newest employees, had the tighter goals. More senior employees had goals such as "Must complete safety training by December 31st." This, of course, is not a goal and it should have been neither written nor signed. Other worthless statements considered 'goals' included "Work hard daily" and "Recertify as a specialist by August 1st." These are not goals. We quickly directed all supervisors to recreate goals and submit them directly to the steering committee for approval. We also recommended that managers throughout the organization randomly select SMART goals for scrutiny.

Employee and supervisor confusion also cause poor SMART goals that may be specific, measurable, attainable, and time-based without being relevant. Employees and supervisors must constantly have relevancy communicated to them from management. Without relevancy, silly and unfocused operations will serve as waste magnets attracting resources they do not deserve. The author has created a better model for creating goals: STRAFOG. STRAFOG is an acronym for Strategy Focused Operational Goals. It is meant to create strategy facing goals. As opposed to SMART goals that are sprayed throughout the organization, STRAFOGs are meant only for operational occupations. STRAFOGs are specific, measurable, attainable, and time-based because they are strategically aligned. STRAFOGs are also relevant because the organizational strategy is relevant. STRAFOG works, and the author encourages organizations to use this when creating goals going forward.

Reward System

It is intuitive that organizations should reward good performance. After the strategic values are communicated and goals are established, it is imperative that achievement is met with rewards. Rewards were covered in detail within the Human Resources chapter. It is important for managers to remember that base compensation is not enough to encourage consistent high performance. High performance employees who realize that low performance employees take home the same check will soon melt into the pack of mediocrity. Motivation is a factor in many organizations. The reward system of that organization is usually a driving cause of both poor performance and poor motivation.

Policies and Procedures

Establishing policies and procedures is an imperative method for removing the guesswork from operations. Expectations are not simply created; they are established from best practices. Policies and procedures allow employees to stay within the boundary of acceptable performance, and this has positive benefits for both the employer and the employee.

Policies

Policies govern the actions of operations specifically and the entire conduct of the organization globally. Organizations should create policies for every department. Startup companies with a single employee should also have policies in place. Policies are the driving factor of business decisions, especially for routine operations. Decisions may include anything, such as how best to repair a pipe and who should receive communication first when a vendor is late with a product. Policies further touch each realm of the business diagram. It is pasted below for reference.

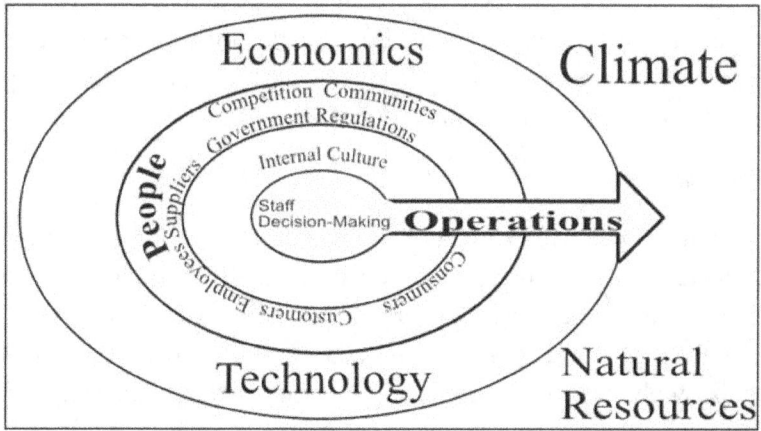

Policies will cover how technology is used in operations. Information technology is an evolving industry, and so too should policies receive consistent updates. Policies will affect the budget, communication with people, operations performed by customers and suppliers, and governmental affairs. Policies add more depth and life to strategic vision and work in a great space between detailing what is expected and how to accomplish this expectation.

Procedures

Procedures give a step by step guide on how to accomplish a specific task, process, or function. Often, policies are created by executive management. It is often lacking the finer details that require it to work. Executive management understands what needs to be accomplished; yet, many do not have the knowledge of how to get from Point A to Point B in every job or discipline. This is not an attack on leadership. It is unrealistic for a senior manager to have detailed knowledge on each position in the organization. Management is charged with organizational decision-making and the strategy is drilled down into a policy for that purpose. Procedures are the work of subject matter experts.

Subject Matter Experts

Subject matter experts, directed by a policies and procedures management team, create a standard operating procedure (SOP) that encapsulates the requirements for a specific task or process. There are no limits as to what qualifies for a standard operating procedure. SOPs have been completed for company phone usage, pipe repair, and company vehicle usage. There are no wrong answers for creating a procedure. It is best that a company is proactive in its approach to creating these documents.

A reactive procedure is usually caused by an employee performing a task that is clearly wrong but who refuses to change because it is in a gray area. Gray area here equates to a lack of written explanation on how best to perform the task. This reactive scenario plays itself out as a manager who had a confrontation with the 'wrong doer', or was silently upset, requests that the policies and procedures team takes a detailed look at this task or process. Obviously, raising this task or process for review will alienate the wrong doer. Proactive SOPs are better; however, reactive procedures are better than frequent improvisation.

Subject matter experts can either have an outgoing personality that looks to assist in any way possible or they can have a shelled personality that looks to protect their 'lane'. Job fright reigns supreme in the hearts and minds of millions of employees the world over. These employees believe that if they explain a task that is important to their job, that anyone could follow them, read it, and perform their job. These employees believe that a key element to them remaining on the organization's roster is their ability to keep their knowledge to themselves.

There are two ways that managers should approach this issue. First, standard operating procedures are indeed for standardizing a task or process. We can conclude from this, that if there was a vacancy in that job that the newly hired employee would decrease her learning curve by reading and learning from the standard operating procedure. However, when she becomes a subject matter expert, she would be expected to add to the procedure as it is updated. Managers obviously cannot diminish the fear of getting fired with the above explanation. Managers can explain that the current employee should be secure in his job. The very fact that he was approached by the organization to be a subject matter expert on a task highlights the high regard that the organization has for the employee and his performance. Encapsulating a process is not a threat. It is an opportunity. An opportunity for subject matter experts to share what they know, to find weaknesses in an aged process, and bring forth solutions for those issues. Several individuals have stood out because of their deep knowledge of a vital process. Management, many times, have taken note and promoted the subject matter expert to a more accountable, and better paying, position because of this knowledge. Managers must communicate this early and often to ensure that procedures are of the highest quality.

Standard operating procedures certainly have checks and balances to ensure their veracity. The organization does not want to find itself hostage to a rogue employee masquerading as a subject matter expert. The policy and procedures team provide a needed balance, that challenges experts to give greater and greater detail and support their procedure with either applicable code, regulations, or data. Code and regulation are applicable to society at large. A water utility cannot have a procedure that conflicts with the standing body of pipe assessment. Those procedures must conform. Data is also a check for these documents. A retail company may assume that a warehouse filled to maximum levels is the best procedure to meet the inventory policy. However, data may prove that just in time (JIT) inventory is more cost effective and more responsible. Employees identified as experts should have their decisions questioned to find the best way forward.

For startup companies and other small firms without many employees, it is important that managers create SOPs for the work that they complete.

Many young firms may use consultants and other contracted labor. This is a great opportunity to contract the creation of an operating procedure. These contractors should have a great knowledge of the work performed and are great resources for standardizing a task or process.

These documents should be accessibly stored. There are some organizations who shield these documents as classified and only release them to the employees whose jobs they directly affect. This is a mistake and shows the ultimate madness of silos and lanes within an organization. Each task has indirect supporters. If an organization is strategically aligned, then all tasks and processes are related in their stated goal of accomplishing the strategic vision. Companies should allow procedure access to all employees and contracted consultants.

Implementation

Implementation is a very important element for procedures. After the procedure has been signed into existence, the policy and procedures team should focus on implementing it through communications and demonstrations with the directly affected parties. This stage is equally important if the standard operating procedure was created or replaced an existing procedure. It is intuitive that a new procedure should be communicated as the steps could be entirely unexpected. However, replacing a procedure carries more stubbornness among vetted employees who will often slide back to old habits.

The author led a policy and procedure team that implemented a software system into the daily tasks of radio dispatchers. These dispatchers, with decades of experience in the position, were now directed to use a system that gave the exact location of jobsites and vehicles, the system told them the distance of each vehicle to the jobsite, the speed of travel, and the accessibility of roads. It was a great system for radio dispatchers to incorporate into their tasks. However, it was difficult for managers to pull the dispatchers from the old method though it was clunky and inaccurate. That system consisted of speaking on a radio, asking where the technician was located, and assigning jobs based on area and not proximity.

There were obvious issues that management found in this original process. First, technicians lie. If they are not feeling up to working, they will state that they are at a jobsite when they are under a bridge resting. Technicians will state that they are finishing up a job when they are in a restaurant enjoying a two-hour lunch break. With the exact whereabouts of the vehicle now known, it made complete sense to use it. Second, by assigning jobs by area and not by availability, we found that the time to complete the job increased significantly and the work was not evenly distributed. If one area of town had intense flooding, the jobs in that area would outnumber the others 20 to 1. This job dumping caused completion times to be skewed as technicians who were free to work were held back because of boundaries. This had to change; and with communication and multiple demonstrations, the radio dispatchers found that the new procedure made their job easier and more convenient.

Implementation and demonstration stretch throughout all procedures. The organization must reach clarity of expectations. A small retail company should walk through how each associate must address customers. A demonstration will have managers performing the greetings before having the associate perform the greetings. This is important, as a wrongly worded insensitive greeting could cost the company a sale at best and brand loyalty at worst. Without this implementation, employees who cause damage will simply state that they did not know better.

A great example of this was a construction truck driver. While on a jobsite, the driver backed up the vehicle and hit a utility pole. This caused massive collateral damage include power outage for a street and the cost of repairing the utility pole that the construction company was forced to cover. The company had recently updated a standard operating procedure that involved ground guides for backing up large trucks. For months, it was documented in the SOP that a ground guide was mandatory for these trucks. And for months that SOP sat on a shelf and in a computer file. That truck driver was never told about the changing procedure. The company suspended the driver and the foreman on the site without pay for this incident. However, that suspension could have been challenged as the new procedure was never communicated with the driver or the foreman. Though the driver did admittedly hit the utility pole and put two dozen homes in the dark for a couple of days, the foreman was not directed to ground guide the driver. The root of the problem was that the procedure was enforced but not communicated. This managerial laziness led to a secret procedure. Let this be clear, it is unethical to punish an employee for not following a secret procedure.

The benefits of carefully planned, executed, and implemented standard operating procedures include less disturbed operations and higher quality of work. It would be great to state that SOPs remove disturbances from operations. Yet, that simply is not true. Emergencies arise as well as disruptive technologies and practices. However, with SOPs in place that are updated regularly, the risk of poor performance is diminished. This leads to higher quality of work. If an organization allows a group of subject matter experts to create or modify a way of performing a task or process, then it has standardized success.

The risk of employees robotically accomplishing tasks is overshadowed by the hope that more tasks are completed successfully. This is a cost-effective measure to balancing work. If tasks are completed exceptionally well by Employee A and ordinarily by Employee E, then there is no incentive for A to share with E. Yes, it may happen if A and E establish a healthy workplace relationship. Oftentimes, A sees the quality of work difference of E as job security. It would make little sense for A to teach E. With the initiation of a procedure, A provides his knowledge with the organization, and the organization provides these best practices with E. E then must meet the new standard. If E still cannot or will not meet this standard of performance, then E will soon require a new employer. This is the magic of procedures. It gradually lifts performance and removes nonconforming employees who are stuck in neutral.

Learning Organization

Managers are encouraged to create learning organizations. These organizations adjust to the changing business environment and use knowledge to offensively compete in their industry. Environments will change often, and companies must adapt to the change and thrive. Small companies have an edge considering the quickness of their adjustment. However, this adjustment is necessary for all companies regardless of size and industry.

Managers determined to weave the culture of learning into the organization should focus on operations, transferring knowledge, and modifying behavior. Operations remains a focus with all management. It is the center of business existence that justifies all current and future behavior. Managers research the operations of competitors for best practices. This is a wider focus of operations that provides a deeper justification for business behavior and strategy. Managers must then communicate their findings with superiors for potential policy and procedure changes. These changes will modify the behavior of employees. The swiftness of this process from research to operations is critical for companies determined to thrive in their industry.

It is also here that the small and medium enterprise has an advantage over the larger corporation. The advantage is highlighted in the relative flatness of small companies. They have fewer employees and the hierarchy is less pronounced in comparison to large companies. The small organization, when communicating a decision, can place every employee in a room and describe the changes and put them into effect. As companies grow, their hierarchy increases in levels and complexity. Silos are created and communication requires greater planning. Seeing communication through to operations becomes more intricate within multi-national organizations.

It is important that the reader recognizes the loop from researching broad industry operations to modifying operational behavior. There must be a loop of verifying that the decision was put into place. Many managers fail in creating a learning organization because they allow their decisions to rest in peace at a podium. They gather everyone around and make a speech and walk back to their office to measure if their speech was effective. That is simply poor management. Once the research is created, staff must order that a standard operating procedure is either created or updated. Communication is given on the adaptation and supervisors are provided expectations on performance. Staff now finds itself back at operations, measuring the effects of the decision.

If the standard operating procedure was updated, this must be highlighted to employees involved in the tasks. Highlighting the changes does not simply include showing the markups on a software system. It is more than that. It must be communicated verbally to show the relevance of the change. The adjustment may be critical to keeping the doors open, and employees must understand that concept to achieve buy-in. The idea of communicating an adjustment in operations is to express its importance while exhibiting an understanding of the current process.

Managers should constantly hone their ability to communicate effectively. For organizational changes, that may bring phobia if they are drastic, it is necessary to show the planned result. If the organization is moving from eight-hour workdays five days a week to ten-hour workdays four days a week, the benefit of reduced time on construction job sites should be communicated. Managers would ensure that technicians understand that there is business value in completing jobs quicker. Staff, understanding that incentivizing behavior is key to increasing performance and acceptance, would emphasize that a new four-day workweek means a constant three-day weekend. The author was part of a team that researched and communicated the above example. The results were more favorable average job lengths, better performance tracked by less rework, and much higher morale. Sure, there were employees who complained that they were now on a shift from Wednesday to Saturday, and that their precious weekend was interrupted. Yet, when given a survey on the new work hours months after the change, less than 5% of technicians wanted to switch back to five-day workweeks. The reason was simple. Regardless of complaints, they loved the three-day weekends that they now enjoy.

Organizations defensively adjust to the changing business environment by conducting three important activities during the research of operations phase of this loop: solve problem, experiment with new approaches, and learn from the organization's experience. It is necessary to solve the problem through consensus after considering multiple new approaches. Experimenting with new approaches exhibits the willingness of management to get it right. These tests can take the form of a pilot project that is controlled during a length of time to determine whether it was successful. Approaches can also endure experimentation through a business process simulator. These simulators allow organization to save both time and money while giving management the confidence to move forward.

The organization's experience, also known as lessons learned, is an important component to decision making in general and learning cultures particularly. Lessons learned should be digitally filed away. These lessons allow employee and management to find what worked best in a process or project. This has a direct effect on learning organizations, and managers should find an approach that is consistent with past successes and organizational strengths.

Procurement

Procurement is the field of getting things into your company that are required for operations. These things can be either products or services. In this section we will cover contracts, selecting a vendor, and vendor performance. Organizations, depending on their size and sophistication will have these tasks departmentalized as Supply Chain or shuffled under the Legal Department. Other organizations have a designated Procurement Department. However, if you have a small company, your procurement will usually consist of you and the person in the mirror. As the sole proprietor or small businessperson, you are responsible for the procurement processes. This fact can become very overwhelming. It is important for managers and businesspersons in flat organizations to understand that support is a phone call away. Allowing an attorney to look over a contract to judge its quality in terms of effectiveness and efficiency is important. It is amateurish for a company to sign a contract that slams them against a brick wall. Your contracts, at best, are win-win scenarios for both the vendor and your company. However, there should be no circumstances when managers execute contracts that either operationally or financially cripple their company.

Planning Contracts

Contracts are sometimes called agreements. In this text, we use mostly contracts to refer to formal documents between both vendor and company. Informal agreements between parties are not extensively covered in this text. The author views them as mostly meaningless. Formal, signed contracts are what matter most in business. The planning of those contracts requires legal knowledge, negotiating skills, and an established procurement process.

Legal knowledge of contracts is dependent on the jurisdiction of the company's operations. This is very inconvenient to search engine warriors. A beautiful contract designed in Liberia may have little or no overlapping relevancy to your area. Managers can do the hard work, or they can delegate it to an attorney. Attorneys are highlighted throughout contract planning because their service is invaluable. Their service should be accompanied by the manager's best judgment.

Negotiating is a great area of business and operations specifically. It involves understanding the needs of the vendors (in this situation) and knowing the demands of your organization. Often, negotiating is a pulling exercise where one side attempts to secure a lopsided victory. Perhaps this idea of domination is instilled in these managers as children when they search for victory during sports or attempt to get the gold stars pinned next to their name in class. Me over you. Us dominating them. We did it. There is a better approach to negotiating: win-win.

When negotiating, managers are encouraged to find the vendor's needs. The need cannot simply be cash and more cash. The vendor may want cashflow extending throughout the next couple of years. Here, you know that the vendor is looking for a longer contract. In some areas, large vendors will receive better contracts if they subcontract with smaller companies or woman-owned companies. This is a need for that vendor. Once managers understand the needs of the vendor, they work to secure the needs of the vendor. The needs of your organization should also be explained. This runs counter to the perspective that your needs should be hidden during negotiation. Hiding your needs is a great way to make the negotiating process long, tedious, and contentious.

Though managers are encouraged to negotiate in good faith, they must remember: my money my rules. It is a simple mantra that organizations must replay during negotiations. This means that managers are not timid when requesting a term because each section of a contract is negotiable. It also means that the company provides the contract to the vendor. The vendor is then given the opportunity to counter any term within that contract.

The author has seen terrible contracts executed into operation. On one instance, the organization "Company A" did not include a timeframe for completing requested service by the vendor. This was, of course, exploited by the vendor who took months to provide the service that Company A requested. As the author took over this contract for Company A, attempts were made to have requests for service completed within five business days. As you can imagine, that attempt was a failure. The vendor had secured a three-year favorable contract and had no incentive to enhance it. It is important for managers of medium and large corporations to understand that the contract may outlive the employment of the person(s) who executed it. These vendors were quite nice as I tried to make the contract work better for our operations. It was not simply reaching an agreement on the time to complete requests but also on how data is stored and shared. As stated, the vendors were well mannered. However, they did not budge. Not an inch. Not a centimeter. Nothing. Good faith is best seen before the contract is executed with signatures. After that, it is a gamble.

Another contract issue occurred not because of poor negotiations, but laziness. The author was purchasing an apartment building and our agent requested that the listing agent send a purchase agreement. This goes against our mantra, my money my rules. So many of our contingencies were left off the contract. It was a mess all wheeled into action because of our agent's laziness. The listing agent even went so far as to write in the name of his banker as the source for our financing. We were now in a position of negotiating this contract instead of the other way around. Perhaps it is obvious, but it is still worth stating that we no longer work with that real estate agent.

The procurement process answers four primary questions:

1. What is needed
2. Should the company make or buy
3. Contract type
4. Vendor pool

Needs of the company

The company should know precisely what they require. This holds true whether the contract is for a service or a product. Contracts cover the scope of business and managers should look at contracts both big and small. In the business community, especially in universities, students and professionals are told about critical thinking. It is a buzzword that has lost some of its sting, but it still holds a place in business orthodoxy. The author remembers sitting in a classroom and hearing that

critical thinking is thinking about thinking. Well, we can do better than that. In this context, a manager should strategically think about all areas of the business with operations at the center. This would resemble a bicycle tire with many spokes. For managers, this means that the locks of the building are an important contract for the safety and risk of operations. Closed circuit television for security is important, and managers understand that how the data is stored is a critical negotiation term. Failure to consider the smaller contracts as important raises the risk of operations. Imagine if a manager spends weeks in negotiation purchasing $1,200,000 in construction equipment but purchases residential locks from a hardware store and has no security system. The organization will have a setback if they find their pitiful locks were snapped like a twig and $350,000 worth of equipment was stolen. The stolen equipment will slow operations. Slowed operations can raise the risk of not fulfilling a contract. All of this could have been avoided if staff considered security and locksmith companies important. When looking throughout the company for potential contracts, remember to think of operations first before identifying the spokes.

Make or Buy

The make or buy decision is an important crossroad for procurement. It is not static, and it does not pertain to each purchase. The buy decision is further drilled down to own or lease. Company policy, as always, is an active element to making this decision. Policy may express that leases are not prohibited. Of course, for small companies, policy can be updated to allow leases. Yet, for large companies, changing a policy is laborious and managers are discouraged from wasting time attempting to change these policies. Managers are encouraged to create a make or buy analysis early in the procurement process. There are three primary factors for the make or buy analysis: capabilities, schedule, and cost.

First is capability. This is an easy decision (most of the time). If you own a construction company, and you are procuring backhoes, the decision could be simple: buy. Your company does not make construction equipment and does not plan on getting into that line of operation. The decision becomes more complicated when an organization has the capability to produce the good or could learn to produce it relatively quickly. An organization producing paper products may determine to procure the same products from a vendor. The cause of this procurement would be a new contract that the organization secured. The company would quickly understand that to fulfill that contract, they would need to purchase a specific amount of paper products. Managers identify the capability of a company by thoroughly examining possibilities with a creative and honest perspective.

Throughout procurement, unilateral decision making should be avoided. Management should work together to create a consensus. For managers to understand what is needed in the organization, they must have conversations, and not only with themselves. Managers must consider each job and speak with the supervisors and managers in each field. If the company is small and flat, this task will take considerably less time than a manager performing the task in a department and division compartmentalized organization. Speak with the janitor and the customer service representative to understand their needs in fulfilling their job tasks.

Bring that knowledge to staff and discuss capability before reaching a decision on buy versus make.

Consulting is another great example of capabilities affecting the decision on whether to make or buy. A business consultant company that approaches your organization to produce strategic reports from your data is clearly providing value. Perhaps your company does not now create these business intelligence reports. However, your company does possess the potential to train certain managers to create the reports. This decision is also affected by the cost consideration. Management may choose to go in both directions by procuring the services of the consultant while also training a staff member. The organization may have foreseen a learning curve and wanted to give the manager time to become proficient in these new systems. Here, the organization would procure the consultant for a one-year period.

The schedule must be considered when considering to either make or buy. In supply chain management lead times are stressed. Lead time is the period required to fulfill an order from purchase to delivery. Customers and consumers are becoming increasingly impatient and time demanding. It is not projected that this will change. Companies should be selected and make or buy decisions must be made while considering lead times. A vendor moving at their own pace could cause the organization to breach their contract.

Cost is nearly always a factor in quality management. Business schools stress quantitative management. A professor once stated that nothing is left if the numbers are removed. This is an extreme idea that places cost over everything. Some managers would debate this piece of business orthodoxy by highlighting the environmentally sound practices and other sustainable organizations with a triple bottom line that considers profits as well as people and the environment. Cost is a factor and it requires quality management to ensure that the organization can open its doors tomorrow to serve more people. However, just like in school when you found out that you can have more than one best friend, managers should also focus on the total value of the company and its procurements by leaving the often toxic paradigm of cash over everything.

For the make or buy decision, it is important that the managers consider the cost of the product or service. If the organization can make a product, it may still choose to procure it externally if a company can produce it cheaper than the organization can make it. This is common in many industries. The cause is that larger companies are usually more efficient in purchasing and producing because of size and experience. An example of this, is a shoe company that found a niche in the trendy clothing market. The founder could have wasted capital by purchasing a shoe making machine. Instead, the entrepreneur purchased basketball shoes in bulk and artistically added value by painting their exteriors. The make or buy analysis was to buy and focus on adding value. The cost of making the shoe would have put a financial burden on the young company and the time required to fabricate a shoe would have been better suited for painting murals that made the artist famous. When considering cost, evaluate the cost of the product and the cost of your labor if the product is an input.

Contract type

There are three main contract types to consider for procurement: fixed price, time and material, and cost reimbursable. Both fixed price and cost reimbursable are covered in detail below. It is important to remember when forming contracts and negotiating that managers should not negotiate vendors on a train track. What could first appear as a victory could later turn to a recurring headache. If the buyer secures a dominate win at the negotiating table, the seller will take actions to save and increase a profit throughout the life of the contract. There are no known companies that play to lose! Non-profit organizations are looking for good deals to stay in business. Petty issues to secure a bigger profit appear less frequently when managers seek to secure the win-win. There are several subtypes of the three main contract types, this text includes some of those subtypes below.

Fixed Price. Fixed Price is a very common contract type that involves well-defined requirements. The seller does not disclose its profits as it simply presents a single cost to the buyer. A subtype of a fixed price contract is the fixed price plus incentive fee. This added incentive fee adjusts profits based on seller meeting specified performance criteria. These criteria are established in the contract and usually is connected to a quicker, cheaper, or better product or service delivery. Incentives are a very power factor for increasing performance.

Fixed price with price adjustments is another subtype of the fixed price contract. This includes a fixed price in addition to a price increase for the cost of material. This is used for a multiyear contract that depends of considerable amounts of material. Sellers like this contract as it protects them from unseen price hikes and lowers their risk throughout the life of the contract.

With a time and material contract, the buyer pays on a per hour or per item basis. This contract type allows for greater control for the buyer. The buyer, for several reasons, determined that a fixed price with this seller is not acceptable. The veil of profit is pierced and the buyer's organization not only views but also controls both the cost per hour and the material cost. This contract is further bound by language that places a ceiling on the total costs. These clauses are put in place to prevent runaway contracts.

Cost Reimbursable. Cost reimbursable contracts are used when the exact statement of work is uncertain. We will cover statements of work further in this chapter. In short, they are the scope of what is expected to be completed during the life of the contract. The buyer organization assumes much of the risk in this contract because future costs are presently contracted. Cost plus fixed fee, cost plus incentive fee, and cost plus fee are a few subtypes of cost reimbursable contracts covered below.

Cost plus fixed fee is intuitive and includes the cost of materials and a profit. That profit is, here, referred to as a fixed fee. Like many of the cost reimbursable contracts, this subtype favors the seller. Cost plus incentive fee is similar to the fixed price plus incentive fee. This subtype adjusts the contract for performance. Managers are targeting the human characteristic to earn more profits by establishing incentives. With incentives in the contract, organizations should conclude that if a performance measure was not reached that the vendor could not reach it. If the vendor could have met the performance criteria and secured the incentive, it would have attained it.

The last subtype for cost reimbursable contracts is the cost plus fee. This is sometimes referred to as a cost plus percentage of costs contract. This is a contract that is rarely used. However, it is great to know and understand. In this subtype, the vendor is paid for costs and a percentage of costs as a fee. If the costs were $100,000, the fee would be $10,000 and the total to the vendor would be $110,000. As you can imagine, this contract is not used often as it incentivizes unethical practices from vendors. This contract requires micromanaging from the buyer. Generally, this subtype is best avoided for a buyer.

The above can be a bit confusing for many. A matrix table is a great way to plainly state the advantages and disadvantages of the three contract types. Cost reimbursable and fixed priced contracts are the most common types and the risk of each should be considered. The cost risk for cost reimbursable contracts leans toward the buyer who assumes more risk than the seller. For fixed priced contracts, the opposite is true, the seller holds a greater cost risk than the buyer. The below tables shows advantages and disadvantages from a buyer's perspective.

Fixed Price

Advantages	Disadvantages
Known price adds security for planning	Statement of work should be detailed, and this places more responsibility on managers to create clear statements for work to be correct
The seller now has an incentive to control price	There is a performance risk for the seller that finds security in a fixed priced contract
There is less need to micromanage this account	

Time and Material

Advantages	Disadvantages
This contract places more control for the buyer	Abuse by the vendor is common in lightly managed time and material contracts
The smaller increments for approval also allude to the greater control	This potential for abuse will require more time micromanaging these contracts by managers
These contracts are created quickly and are usually brief in nature. This allows the buyer flexibility in either extending or ending the relationship	

Cost Reimbursable

Advantages	Disadvantages
A major advantage of this contract type is the inherent built in control	Abuse by the vendor is regular and buyers should expect this. This will require that buyers audit costs
The high emphasis on incentives squeezes the best performance out of vendors	
Cost reimbursable contracts require simpler statements of work in comparison to fixed priced contracts. This eases the responsibility and burden from managers	
Generally, these contracts are cheaper than fixed priced contracts	

Statement of Work

Statement of work (SOW) is mentioned several times in this text. It is an important element of the contract, without it, the contract would consist of signatures and wishes for the outcome. The statement of work is the primary body of the contract. It is clear, concise, and describes a job well done. Vendors should be able to look at a SOW and understand what is expected of them if they win that contract.

A poor SOW can cause overspending, rework, and litigation. These are three areas that companies, and small companies particularly, should avoid. Overspending is a result of poor management. Rework, a common cause of ambiguous statements of work, is a cost drain on the company. For internal work, it will lead to frustration and a decline in morale. For contracted labor and materials, it may lead to litigation. There are few places that small companies dread more than a courtroom. It is a direct pull on precious resources. Many small companies do not have an attorney on their roster and this attorney fee will put a spotlight on the poorly constructed SOW.

Vendor Pool – Bid Documents

The statement of work is a direct input into the bid document. The bid document is communicated with potential vendors. It includes information about the company, the SOW, procedures for winning the contract, selection criteria, and proposed terms and conditions among other elements. This is an important document. This is the moment when internal efforts are communicated externally. This is when vendors get a window into the organization. There are four primary bid documents:

request for proposal (RFP), request for quote (RFQ), invitation to bid (IFB), and request for information (RFI).

The request for proposal is the most widely used bid document for large contracts. RFPs request detailed proposal price, the experience of the vendor, how the statement of work will be accomplished, and who will do it. The next three bid documents are usually less detailed than the RFP. The RFQ requests a quote per item or unit of measure. The invitation to bid (IFB) is also called a request to bid (RFB) and it is a request for the total price to do all required work. The RFI can be used prior to another bid document. With the RFI, the buyer gains knowledge on the qualification and capabilities of vendors.

The results of good bid documents include a larger volume of responses, more accurate pricing, and more intuitive comparison of responses. Poorly worded bid documents and confusing performance measures create inertia in vendors. Vendors will either ignore the request and not bid or throw together a poorly constructed bid to match the unprofessional bid document. A concise bid document encourages suppliers to bid with the hope of not simply earning the contract but also working with a quality company.

Accurate pricing is another benefit of a responsible bid document. Inaccurate pricing is a result of unclear statements of work. If vendors are confused of what is required in material and time, they typically round up. By communicating a clear format for bids, the organization ensures that managers spend less time analyzing responses. As managers plan the organization's procurement, it is imperative that they look to save time. A small company with three managers should avoid having one spend three months on a single procurement. This is a quarter of the entire year. A great way to cut time is to have an accurate and concise bid document that does not require rework and manages the format of incoming vendor responses.

Evaluation and Selection

This section of the procurement process includes conducting the bidder conference, receiving and evaluating vendor responses, facilitating vendor presentations, negotiating, and executing the contract. At a glance, this section may appear lengthy. It does not need to take months. This entire section should be planned before the bid document is release and should take no more than a few weeks when properly executed. The author has seen this section expand to several months of negotiations in a display of misled management. Managers should look to plan and control procurement and not prolong any process. When organizations prolong processes, they lose hours of precious resources.

Bidder Conference

The bidder conference is set for potential sellers to ask questions after receiving the bid document. The answers to these questions are added as addenda to the bid document. This bidder conference can be a physical meeting or a teleconference. Often it is a combination of both. The facilitator of this conference should ensure that each vendor has the opportunity to express concerns and ask questions. Any question that the facilitator cannot answer, should be researched, added to the addenda, and sent to all bidders.

Receiving and Evaluating Vendor Responses

The buyer organization states the due date for proposals and bids. Once the procurement manager receives the proposal, a predetermined evaluation committee begins the critical work to select a vendor. The evaluation committee begins by screening out obviously unqualified sellers that do not meet minimum requirements. The second step is to use predetermined source selection criteria to further narrow the bidder group. The source selection criteria are usually weighted to past performance and experience and independent cost estimates. The cost estimates are established to manage expectations and highlight blatant outliers. These evaluations will either lead to vendor presentations or directly to negotiations.

Vendor Presentations

Vendor presentations are important if they are facilitated correctly. Letting a salesman stand up and hold forth for an hour can be a boring disaster. The vendor should understand that technical questions will be asked and the appropriate staff should be present to answer those questions immediately. Presentations are especially critical for complex work. Complex work includes new software systems and integrations of systems that will require a project before operations. After the presentation, the evaluation committee will score the presentation by predetermined metrics. This is important because it is usually the last step for ranking companies and before moving into negotiations.

Negotiating and Executing the Contract

Negotiations should end with a contract and a strong professional relationship. Firstly, it is not required in fixed priced contract types. The buyer organization should negotiate for fair and reasonable prices. The three main items to negotiate are scope, schedule, and price. They do not move in unison. If your organization pushes for tighter scope and a quicker schedule, expect to pay more. If your organization is cost conscious and looks to save, expect the scope to decline in negotiations. Other common items that are negotiated are quality, payment schedule, and responsibilities. Once negotiations are finished and the contract is executed, the buyer organization should store the contract electronically and have a small gathering to celebrate a job well done.

Controlling Contracts

It would be great if both parties followed the executed contract letter for letter. Perhaps in this utopian world, the managers of both organizations would share a coffee break each Friday. In the real world, disputes happen. Many times, the disputes arise from honest mistakes that require correction. Other times, the disputes are intentional and unethical. The human spectrum is both awesome and pitiful.

Managers should focus their attention on several recurring issues in contract management. First, vendors who perceive that negotiations ended in the buyer's favor will look for ways to increase their profit. At times, the vendor was not wronged but instead used a low unrealistic price to secure the contract. In these situations, the managers should watch for an inflated contingency budget. This is the budget that pays for unexpected expenses. The author was a project manager on a construction project that signed a contract with a lowballing company. Within the first month, the company began pulling at the contingencies. Our company learned the hard way, that a cheaper offer does not make it the best offer. Companies that use this tactic are unethical. Contingencies are for foreseen and unexpected expenses not for hidden profits.

A second issue that managers must stand on guard for is the unincentivized seller. Back in our world of utopia, we will find vendors who are motivated that they secured a valid contract. These utopia vendors want to deliver at scope, on schedule, and under cost because their name and reputation are on the line. Now back in reality, many companies lose interest in yesteryears contract after they sign a new contract. Symptoms of the unincentivized seller is garbage and higher prices. These vendors begin to step on the scope and quality for speed and ease and to save money. They will also overprice any requested change in the contract.

Scope creep is a third issue that is especially relevant for companies that use time and material contracts. Vendors, paid for their time will naturally attempt to stretch the schedule and exaggerate their efforts.

What your organization should do when the vendor is not following the contract is subjective. Business orthodoxy demands that the company immediately terminate the contract for a breach. Above, I stated that some breaches of contract are honest mistakes. In these situations, an organization that terminates the contract is overreacting. It is the authors suggestion that vendors receive a stern written warning for minor breaches. Termination of the contract should follow this warning. Of course, if unethical practices are detected, then the business relationship needs to have an abrupt ending through contract termination.

Procurement is an unavoidable section of operations. Companies require contracts and professional relationships for a variety of reasons. The supply chain into your company should be seamless and without hurdles. That is possible in a utopian world. In the business arena, companies will need to manage vendors who look to cut corners to unfairly secure greater profit.

Information Technology

Information technology is an important component in sophisticated operations. Technology and innovation are expansive and shape both organizations and industries. This segment of the text will highlight some basic concepts of storage and management of data. Data visualization as a communication tool is also explained with the hopes that the reader takes advantage of current available tools.

Data Storage

There was a time that handwriting sales was the norm. That time has passed. Most small businesses use a spreadsheet saved on a single computer and shared when necessary. Spreadsheets are a great start to exceptional data storage. However, as the company becomes larger and sales increase, the use of a database will become important for storage needs of the organization. Databases store more information and allow greater manipulation of data.

Database management systems (DBMS) connect with databases to create meaningful reports for decision making. These systems provide intuitive reports that management requires for further analysis. As business owners and managers, pertinent and timely information is key to swift and accurate decisions. This leads to the idea of quality inputs into your database, spreadsheet, or notebook. The demand of quality inputs has not changed with the development of software. Many know this as Garbage In Garbage Out (GIGO). When using a DBMS, the author queried to find the difference in time between the start and finish times for a specific group of jobs. The averages were off. It did not take long to find that several of the finish times were incorrectly inputted into the database. They were inputted as occurring before the start time. Quality data entry is the nucleus for quality database management systems.

Once the erroneous data was set aside, the author was able to discover and report the average times spent on similar jobs broken down by technician. This performance information will affect operations. Managers, now with a window into performance, and with the data to support assumptions, could now create additional measures and exceptions for technicians.

Data Management

Databases also work with customers. Sophisticated companies care about customer information. There is no flexibility here. All managers and business owners must care about, among a myriad of factors, what person or company is purchasing their goods and services, when they are purchasing them, and where they reside. In the below example, Lori Sandals discovers how best to serve its clients.

Lori Sandals is an online store selling handmade sandals made of wood and leather. These sandals are environmentally friendly and Kori, the business owner, has found that over the past 12 months, her hobby has become a business. She put away the spreadsheet for a database. She connected a database management system to provide meaningful reports. Kori is at her table with a cup of coffee when she begins querying the system. She has not yet employed a report developer, so she is completing these tasks herself with the help of a consultant that Lori Sandals contracts hourly when needed.

Lori Sandals is based in Ohio. Kori markets mostly to the Southwest region of the United States. She believes, from handling the orders, that the majority of the sales are in that region. However, the increase in sales has converted this estimate into a blur. Now she will get the definitive answer. Over the past 12 months, 40% of her sales were in Florida, not the Southwest. Only California in the Southwest made purchases totaling 20% of all sales. New York, Maryland, Pennsylvania, and New Jersey in the East accounted for the remaining 40%. Further, Kori discovered that primary sales in California were to retail companies. While the majority of the sales in Florida, New York, Maryland, Pennsylvania, and New Jersey were to end-users. All of this information was significant for Kori and she made the decision to reposition Lori Sandals to target the areas that are most loyal to her brand.

The above is an example of the power of information. Databases, spreadsheets, and notebooks all contain data. If Kori had handwritten all of her sales in the past year, it would have taken her a weekend to make sense of that pile of data. Data should follow a natural progression to information then to knowledge, and finally to wisdom. Data by itself is useless. It must be interpreted and used to shape the operational behavior of the organization.

For many managers and small business entrepreneurs, technology is a feared word. During extensive trips to Kenya, it was explained to the author that elephants in the area ran from the color red. In fact, it was a learned behavior that served as a survival tactic for avoiding Masai warriors who customarily wear red tunics. Their behavior is so rigid that these elephants panic when a non-threatening pedestrian walks nearby with a red shirt. This is the reaction of many professionals and tradesmen when the word technology enters into a conversation. They freeze. They panic. They put up a wall. Obviously, technology is a huge world with many beneficial components. The above text on data storage and management is an important step in allowing IT to work for your company. It is also simple to enter data into a database and generate rudimentary reports. As with our above elephant, the reader must not fear habitually.

Data Visualization

Data Visualization is an important tool of communication. You have the data entered into a database, perhaps you generate summaries detailing operations with specific parameters. Yet, it is the visualization that brings it to life and it is that lively visualization that the reader retains. Information visualization has been around for thousands of years. Early humans passed data-backed messages to others through cave paintings. Surveyors created maps to communicate virgin lands to investors and public administrators back home. W. E. B. DuBois, a known scholar and civil rights leader from the United States, also visualized data before computers. In 1900, his works, along with Atlanta University, detailed the current and historical situation of African Americans throughout the nation. He compiled this stellar research with dozens of hand-drawn and beautifully colored graphs. W.E.B. DuBois communicated these graphs internationally in Europe and America.

The old adage that a picture is worth a thousand words holds true with data visualization. Imagine putting a book of written information, two inches thick, before a crowd of interested onlookers. It is apparent, that only those with the strongest interest will go through the book. Compare that with a gallery of graphs that several viewers can digest simultaneously. W.E.B. DuBois, with neither databases nor computers, created a lasting and historically important work that has stood the test of time. The modern businessperson and manager cannot leave the tools of data collection, storage, manipulation, and visualization for the next organization to exploit. Allow the visualization to speak a thousand words for your organization.

Data visualization is also great when constructing a business plan. Yes, there should be some words involved. However, the 50-page business plan is a chore for the reader; whether that reader is a private investor or an employee at a financial institution. The author was recently contracted to create a business plan by an operating alterations company for the purpose of securing an investment. After requesting and gathering important data, it was entered into a database. The business plan comprised of several important and key information visualizations that not only detailed the current state of the company but projected future revenue among other metrics. The business plan was easy to read and the business owner was more than satisfied with the purchased product. The business owner did not know to ask for visualization; the author is unsure if he understood the necessity of a database. However, the goal of communicating information is usually best with graphics. Business plans should excite and inspire, and if it used for investment, it should also persuade in the simplest and clearest way possible.

Project Management

Projects are a great way to expand current operations. Projects are often confused with operations. They are not. Projects are activities with a planned start and finish date to produce a unique product, service, or result. Projects, and their management, are covered in this operations chapter because they are still part of operations. This is seen in project management orthodoxy with programs, the next higher level of project organization, consisting of both projects and operations. For maturing and growing companies, managers should plan to conduct project management consistently. This section of the text is an overview of project management.

The author is a licensed project manager, with four internationally recognized designations, and several years of managing projects in three countries. The above is stated not to rank myself on a nonexistent list. Instead, the author wishes to convey the importance of hiring qualified project managers. This section will point you in the right direction, yet an experienced project manager will bring dreams to life through project activities.

In the following pages, the reader will learn about a project charter, how to define the scope, and creating the schedule and budget. The text covers identifying risks, categorizing risks, and planning how best to respond to them. The control of the project through scope and quality are highlighted as important elements of project management. Finally, closing activities and projects are explained in detail. Amateurish project management costs organizations billions of dollars annually. Accidental project management, so common that it became a regularly used term, is the occurrence of an employee assuming project leadership responsibilities without planning and usually without qualification. This is either the result of poor planning or poor human resources. As the employee is forced to run through a dark room, they inevitably hit walls and tables. This text should convince the business owner that skilled project management saves cash and increases the probability of success.

Business Case and Project Charter

The business case is not a long document. Yet, it is powerful in initiating the idea of a project to produce change in an organization. Business cases are created by organizations to justify a proposed project. Projects start here with intense questioning on desirability, viability, and achievability. Desirability questions examine the cost, risks, and benefits of the project. The costs are professional estimates of taking the project from start to finish and delivering the unique product, service, or result. In short, it is the cost of the proposed benefits. The benefits are change. For projects, change is a key qualifier. If the project does not produce change, it is not a project at all. All projects carry an element of risks. Further, those risks can either be attached to the project or to a certain activity within the project. The risks, like the costs and benefits, must be continuously examined and scrutinized throughout the life of the project.

The viability of the project questions whether the project can actually deliver the product, service, or result. Achievability examines if the project can provide the benefits that it claimed. Many projects are little more than sacred cows ordered by executives. This is true for both small and large organizations. There are several mechanisms to stop these projects from going forward and wasting organizational resources. Unfortunately, many small companies do not have these mechanisms that shield organizations from baseless unilateral decisions. These mechanisms include the murder board, scoring, and constrained optimization methods. This text will examine the first two mechanisms.

Selection

The origin of bad projects is varied, but their execution is usually the cause of poor selection procedures. These projects arise seemingly on command upon the hire of a new executive or after a manager attends a conference. In the latter scenario, it is expected that managers learn when in conferences. However, it is imperative that these managers reshape their newfound education and not simply regurgitate their findings in the form of a new project. It is cause for concern when senior managers decide to dramatically shift strategy because of a groundbreakingly awesome tear-rendering conference in paradise. Selection mechanisms protect the organization from unilateral changes through managerial consensus.

The murder board is a great process that tries to 'murder' a project idea before it can be initiated. The murder board is fun yet serious. One person goes to the board and presents the idea of a project while many other board members throw intuitive and hypothetical questions at the presenter. The presenter answers to the best of her ability. A true sacred cow, a hideous project beloved by its creator for personal reasons, should be easily sacked here. Projects that are minefields of misery will fail when answering questions on desirability, viability, and achievability. These projects usually have costs and risks that outweigh benefits. The probability of these projects delivering the product, service, or result is low. At times, the idea that these projects can provide the stated benefits cannot be defended. The murder board is always a great place to start for organizations selecting quality projects.

Scoring and ranking projects requires consistency. The project selection committee, consisting of the same individuals who conducted the murder board, rank projects using predefined criteria. From experience, managers must pay special attention to external influence during project proposal scoring. Managers who sponsored a proposed project will not waste time influencing the scoring committee members. There should be an organizational understanding that this committee is off-limits to such behaviors. Conversations and decisions during project selection, as with vendor selection, should be closely guarded. The information is on a need to know basis. Managers must trust the process that the organization relies upon when selecting the best projects available. The three main areas that are scored, often disguised behind many masks, are costs, risks, and benefits. Decisions are communicated formally. The details of how the decision was reached should be kept for explanation to project sponsors.

Only after the business case has been justified can the project idea move forward. The project is now finding shape, and in the next activity, the project will reach another important milestone. Yet, before the project charter can be created, the project manager must be selected. If you are a small company, take notes and fight the battle of experience with knowledge. If you are a medium or large organization, a seasoned project manager should be onboarded to raise the probability of project success. The unassuming accidental project manager just will not do when serious benefits and risks are at stake. A project manager will take over the project from this point, charter, to the close of the project.

Project Charter

Project Charter is also called the project brief and its purpose is to incrementally add detail to a very cursory business case and to fill in other gaps. Project management, in this way, consists of incremental planning in phases of acceptance. First is the business case with its very cursory explanation of costs, risks, and benefits for justification. Next is the project charter and finally there is a project plan with dynamic and precise details. Whereas the business case is created by the sponsor for the organization's acceptance, the project charter is created by the project manager for both the sponsor and organization's acceptance.

The charter will provide high level details of the project's costs, risks, and benefits. It will also identify stakeholders and give an idea about how they are connected to the project. The area of stakeholders, though drilled down at a later date, receive important focus here as categories of stakeholders are formed. Stakeholders are identified by how they affect the project. This is important for managers to consider and the sometimes technically correct answer of "Well, everyone is a stakeholder," should be avoided. Employers and vendors are an easy place to start when compiling a list of stakeholders. This list is dynamic and does not require a week to set, give it some thought over an hour or so and the stakeholders will organically appear. Customers and consumers are also stakeholders. The community at large is another. A compiled list of stakeholders is an input for characterizing each category.

Stakeholders should be accurately rated under the metrics of both involvement and influence. Stakeholders can be rated high under both and likewise low on either. A matrix chart should be formed to keep track of the findings and easily share among the team. If you are in a flat organization with less than 10 individuals, you will enjoy an advantage in agile communications. For large, virtual, and multi-national organizations, an internal communication plan is a critical piece of project management. Once involvement and influence are created, a communication plan can be established. Stakeholders with the most involvement and influence are communicated with regularly, other stakeholders may only receive an email during project milestones if they are not involved in the project and have little influence over the project's success. This process is subjective and highlights the dichotomy of project management: art and science. It also underlines the importance of dynamic project management, if it is not working, analyze and change.

The project managers must also find the assumptions of each stakeholder. Assumptions are what they believe true about the project. This is a very important step that is often overlooked resulting in abandoned and failed projects. If critical stakeholders believe that a project will deliver benefit

X, but you plan for it to deliver benefit Y, you should look to resolve this immediately. The resolution may be to stop the project before it goes any further. An incorrect assumption from a stakeholder introduces additional risk into the project.

Perhaps more than anything, at least for the project manager, the charter provides official authorization to begin. When organizations give the green light, they also give the green light to use resources. The financial capital and physical equipment to undertake the project successfully is committed at this stage. This is not a blank check. Organizations still reserve the right to end a project that is either ran terribly or whose benefits are no longer justified.

Planning a Project

In theory, project managers now select their teams. This may not always hold true. For small organizations, the project team may be the entire organization and work may be delegated based on amateurish ideas of availability. For larger companies, teams will be selected before detailed planning and will exist for the life of the project before they fade away back into their divisions and departments. Other companies will contract consulting firms to run projects. Accidental project managers find work dumped on their desk with the expectation that success will follow. Business orthodoxy states that organizations cannot do what they cannot plan. In reality, organizations fail their way to success daily. The idea of establishing responsible project management leadership and processes is to reduce risk and focus on the higher probability of success.

There are many steps in project management. There are a few bodies throughout the world that prescribe to a certain and set process. The author is a member within many of these bodies. Allow the above to preface the acknowledgment that this is not a minutely detailed project management text. The purpose of this text, besides expanding on operations, is to teach managers project management theory to permit them to better manage project managers.

Project Scope

Creating a scope is the next important process for project management. It is important for the scope to be unpacked into a collection of requirements. The requirements are carefully considered and brought together before the project manager through a variety of methods. Teams brainstorm and interview stakeholders to narrow down on requirements. Those that are outside of the established charter are rejected. Requirements that support the stated benefits remain to provide foundation for the scope. The affinity map is a great way to map requirements. A silent brainstorm, an activity where team members write all ideas on note cards and compile them without order after a predetermined time. The team then creates groups and places each idea into a group. There will be ideas that are well outside of scope. Some ideas will be outside of reality. There will be duplicates. Eventually, the completed affinity map will support other tools creating a list of requirements and compiling those requirements into a charter supporting scope.

The requirements will lead to a product scope which then leads to a project scope. There are tons of terms in project management. However, the above is simple. The product scope consists of the requirements related to the product, service or result. Remember, a project is a unique product, service, or result. The project scope highlights the work that the team performs to deliver the product. In this way, the product scope is the 'What' and the project scope is the 'How'. Together, the product and project scopes, along with assumptions and other information will form the project scope statement. For non-project managers, this may seem like worthless chatter. The reader may believe that the author dragged him through the weeds. However, the project scope statement is important in gaining approval from stakeholders before further work is completed on the project. Project management is iterative in that it moves step by step. It is not a sprint from start to finish without oversight. Professional project management is a calculated marathon to success.

Project Schedule

With the scope completed, the organization now knows what it hopes to accomplish and the general concept of how to achieve it. This idea of what and how is not only drilled down from business case to charter to project management plan, but it is also consistently verified throughout the life of the project. Creating the dynamic schedule is the next necessary step in planning for the project. The schedule is dynamic in that it is expected to change to meet and adjust to risks. The schedule is created not simply as a box to check, but as a way to make a reasonable and practical path for success. At its core, the schedule is a series of activities organized intuitively to achieve benefits and reduce risks.

Some readers may require visual learning. The below figure shows the process of project management from business case through what is known as the triple constraints: scope, schedule, and budget. Use the below figure as a reference for project management planning.

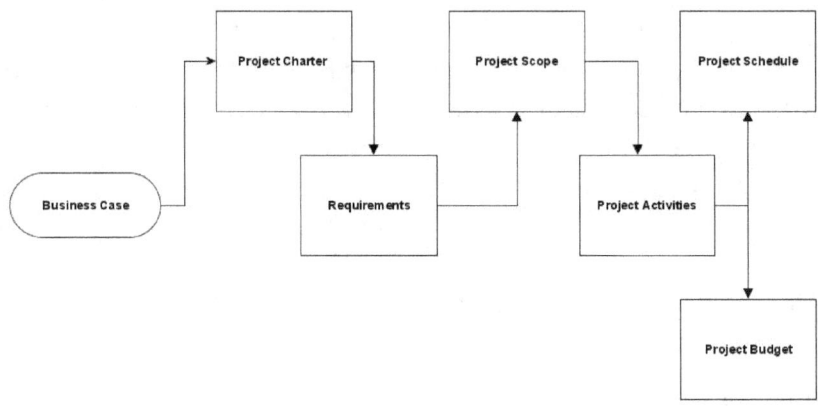

Activities should be logical in their development. They consist of tasks that culminate with a verifiable outcome. The project manager should have the capacity to determine if an activity was indeed successful and its impact on the entire project. If an activity does not have a significant impact, its appearance in the project should be strongly scrutinized. Project managers are also cautioned from digging too deep. An example of an irrelevant activity is a team that is building a software product that puts an activity to sweep and mop the hallways daily. This is irrelevant to the product. If the custodian missed a day, or a week, of cleaning the project would not be thrown off of schedule, budget, or scope.

Once activities are defined, they are sequenced with a network diagram. A network diagram is a major step in creating a schedule, in fact it is a major step in creating a project. There are a few tools that assist in creating a schedule. This text will concentrate on a technique called precedence diagramming method (PDM). The name is not necessary, we will simply refer to it as the network diagram. It is important because of its use of nodes that represent activity showing its estimated time to completion and its dependency on other activities through simple arrows. It is easy to create, read, and interpret. The project manager reading this will agree that this technique is useful. Accidental project managers and other managers will find that it simplifies the schedule building process. Entrepreneurs should read the texts on schedules and immediately see projects in the near future. If you are in the middle of a naïve project, add all that you learn to the project in progress.

There are four types of node relationships that should be understood for this schedule development.

1. Finish to start
2. Start to start
3. Finish to finish
4. Start to finish

These relationships are all defined in their name and are quite intuitive. Yet, for clarity, the reader will find descriptions of each below. Finish to start is a relationship where activity B cannot begin until activity A is completed. A graphic below helps explain this relationship. This is the most common node relationship in project management.

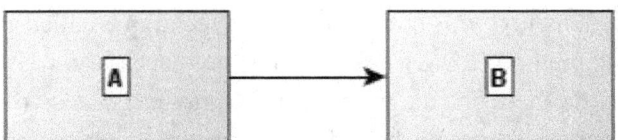

Start to start is a node relationship that allows activity B to begin when activity A begins. This is a great time saving relationship. The clue to start to start is ensuring that activity B is not dependent on an output of activity A. If building software, the activity to build a feature must be completed before testing. In that example, this relationship would not work. However, if you are constructing a building pouring cement could have a delayed start to start node relationship with laying reinforcement bars. The below graphic explains this further.

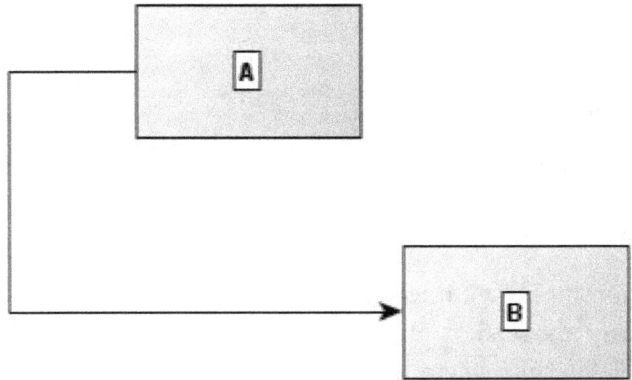

Finish to finish is a relationship that requires activity A finishes before activity B can complete. These activities may appear to have no dependency; yet, a project manager will find that activity B requires an

166

output of activity A to complete. That dependency may be a finish to finish relationship. The graphic below captures this node type.

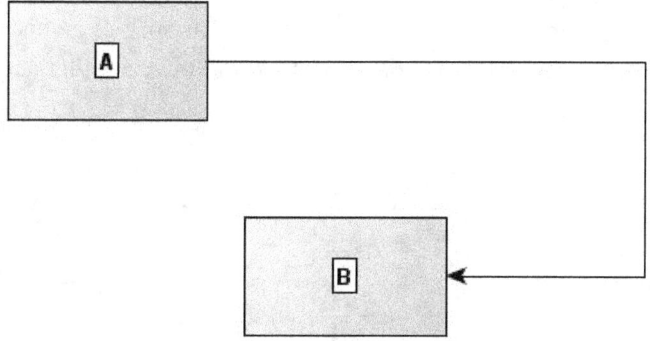

The last and least used relationship is start to finish. Here, activity A must start before activity B completes. It is rare to require this node type. It is useful when details are not fully known and the team approaches the project with flexibility. The graphic below provides illustration to this node type.

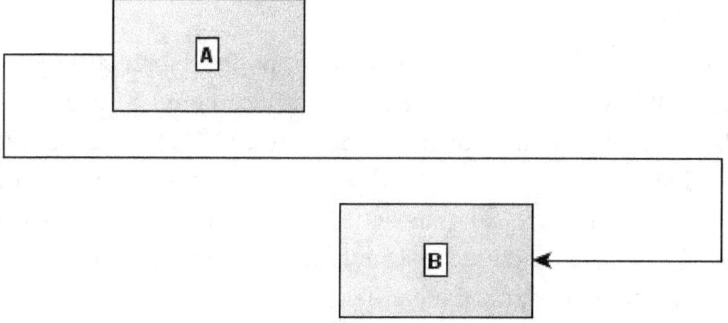

Once, activities are created and relationships are determined, the network diagram will look similar to the below. Notice that an activity, D, has two arrows pointed at it. This means that, in this example, D cannot begin until both activities A and B are complete. Activity E is special in this diagram, as it is the only activity that is permitted to begin once another activity (C) starts.

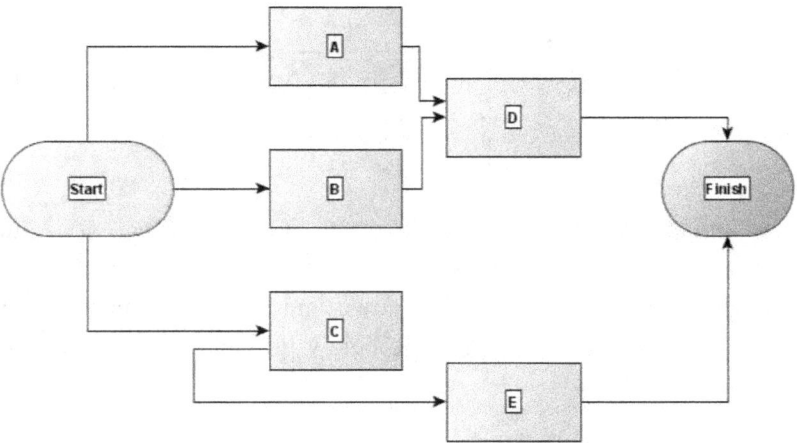

There are scores of project management terms for reference and this text will not make any attempt to relay or define them. However, a few important terms that a manager should understand when creating a schedule include: lag, float, and critical path. A lag is the amount of time between the completion of one activity and the start of a dependent activity. Lags should be used sparingly as it implies that neither activity can be conducted. Imagine a metal fabrication that is molded at scolding

168

hot temperatures. It may be necessary for it to cool to a certain temperature before the next activity can start. This is an example of a lag.

Floats allude to the cushion of time that allows a schedule to have flexibility. There are three types of float: total, free, and project. The total float is the amount of time that an activity can be delayed without delaying the project. The project float is the amount of time that the project as a whole can be delayed without causing schedule creep. The free float is the cushion of time from one activity to its dependent activity. The free float is important, because once it is exhausted there can be a domino effect that forces the entire project to be delayed.

The critical path is the longest path in a project network diagram. The paths are the sequence of arrows that attach one node to another. From the above diagram, it is impossible to determine the critical path as there are no durations in the activity nodes. The critical path highlights itself, there are no formulas. It is the management of a critical path that showcases the skill level of project managers.

With those definitions at the fore and with the defined activities sequenced into a network diagram, the manager now estimates the duration of each activity. There are several methods for this estimation: one-point, three-point, parametric, bully, and more. Bully estimates come from outside of the project management team. It sometimes hides behind past parametric estimates. Parametric estimates are mathematical equations and consider historical performance for probable activity durations. The project management team should be careful of garbage inputs that produce garbage outputs. One-point is a single guess at the duration. It is usually found in accidental project management and can be the output of frustration. Planning a project can be grueling, especially if you are bewildered. In such a scenario, the project manager just looks at the activities and arbitrarily assigns durations to them. When the project team looks unsure about the method, the project manager usually says something such as 'Well, we can adjust if we have to.' That is closer to a roller coaster than a project. Three-point is perhaps, along with parametric, the best method for estimating activity duration. Three-point consists of three estimates for each activity: best case scenario, most probable, and worst case scenario. These times are then summed and divided by three to get an average. Whatever is used, be consistent. It is exhausting and confusing for team members to consider a one-point on one activity a bully on another and a three-point on the last.

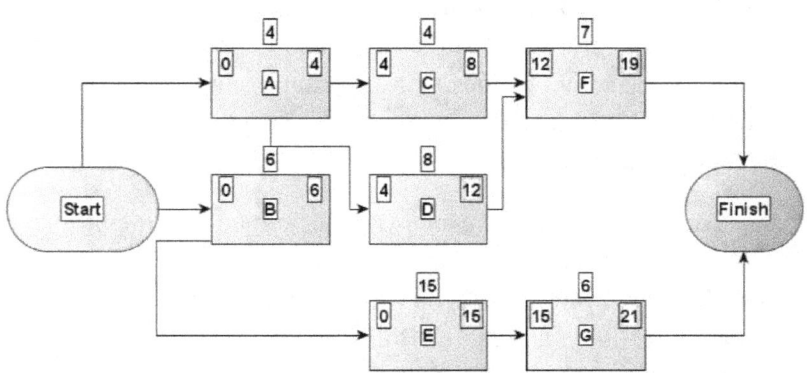

The above network diagram has more information that a project team can use to further shape their efforts. The number above the nodes, the 4 above the A and the 6 above the B, are the durations of that activity. In reality, your activities should have a name and not a letter. Giving activities letters and numbers, and having the name of that activity stored somewhere else adds to confusion and slows the project. Anyone should be able to look at the diagram and understand the natural flow of the project. The left number inside of the node is the earliest start that the activity can begin. This start added to the duration provides the right number inside of the node, the expected completion of the activity.

There are two primary paths in this project:

1. A to C and D, and C and D to F
2. B to E to G

The critical path, explained earlier as the longest path in duration, is B to E to G. The duration of this path, 21 days, is the duration of the project. Therefore, a delay on this path will result in a delay of the project, that is why its management is critical. This is your basic schedule for a project. This schedule, based from the scope, leads into the budget. The network diagram is one of the most important graphics in project management and is a central component to many other elements of project planning, execution, and control.

Project Budget

The best way to create the project budget is by examining the network diagram and considering each activity individually. The budget of a project is little more than the cost of each activity along with a contingency. The estimating techniques for finding an activity's cost is the same for determining activity duration: bully, one-point, parametric, and three-point.

The project manager is ultimately responsible for the project; its ability to achieve scope, stay on schedule, and remain within the budget. Therefore, bully input from outside of the project team should be resisted. Obviously, most project managers are employees and most bully input has an origin of higher rank. This has to be discarded. Project managers protect their reputation and that of the organization and project team. The author is alluding to the strength in character to say 'No'. The project manager must, more often than expected, refuse external input in a brave attempt to shield the project's integrity. The author has served within project management teams where decisions were made by a highly qualified team only to have that decision replaced with external input – insert chief or director. In this instance, the senior project manager never found the courage to say 'No'. Instead, he constantly replaced our plans, reached by expert level consensus, with the plan of a single bully. Needless to say, the project manager lost the respect of the team members. In addition to less respect for the project manager, the other negative affect of bully estimates is expanding the time of the project. Perhaps, time would be saved if the bully gives all estimates immediately. However, the reader should not expect this to occur. The bully, in love with himself, will wait for the most dramatic moments to glide in and provide solutions. They will change your activity duration after you submit it, they will challenge your budget after it is completed. Be ready to stand up and fight back!

One-point should be used sparingly. When project teams provide a one-point estimate, the budget is usually much higher than required. Parametric is a good technique, especially if the organization has completed a similar project. Three-point remains a powerful tool in most situations. The estimates should be researched and not simply yelled out in a meeting.

The costs must consider the things and people to accomplish the activity. These things and people are collectively known as resources. This step is another approval milestone for the project. Since business case, rough estimates have been provided for the cost of the project. The budget is not a rough estimate. The entire project can be stopped and closed immediately if the budget is unfavorable. For amateurish management, the idea of cancelling before completion, or even executing, may seem like a waste of time and resources that contributed to planning. However, these are sunk costs. Sunk costs are past expenses incurred. Sunk costs are not considered when determining how to move forward. A project with costs that outweigh benefits, at any stage, should be terminated immediately.

A mistake that many managers make is not considering the cost of human resources. Organizations do this in general and on projects specifically. This means that there is a cost to that meeting about a meeting. Project managers, in order to be as accurate as possible, should know the current hourly cost of each team member. Usually, the project manager does not know and does not inquire with human resources. Not compiling the cost of team members is amateurish. This is a consistent and large portion of the project's cost and should be thoroughly considered.

Another cost that is sometimes overlooked is the cost of currently owned equipment. The project management team needs to give each piece of equipment an hourly cost. If the backhoe or truck was not on the project it is presumed that it would be put to use on a different activity. This concept also holds true for compiling the cost of team members. The organization must reach an accurate cost to determine if this project has true justification: if its benefits truly outweigh its costs. Not considering the cost of people employed by the company nor equipment owned by the company but listing the cost of leased equipment and contracted consultants will present a lopsided budget that is inaccurate and biased against the organization's best interests.

The project has reached an awesome milestone with this preliminary budget consisting of the compiled cost of resources for each activity. If the project ran smoothly and the project management team had perfect foresight, this would be enough. However, projects are both art and science. The art of project management is witnessing how project managers identify risks, plan their responses, and implement those risk responses. We will cover risks shortly, but it is important to understand that the costs to implement risk responses is considered contingency reserves. This contingency is added to the preliminary budget to create the final budget.

Contingency should 'burndown' if unused. As the project progresses, and activities A and B are completed and closed, their contingency should drop off of the budget. This is a very important area for managers to manage. For projects utilizing third party services, organizations should keep a careful eye on the contingency section of a budget and how that money is requested. A proposal for a service, whether the service is performed by an internal or external team, should never have a blanket contingency plan. For example, a retail operation building an extension on their existing building puts together a team for the project. The project management team gives a budget, $250,000. The organization requests more information. The project management team gives a breakdown, $150,000 for the project and $100,000 contingency. When the organization's manager requests further information on the contingency, the project management team stalls before admitting that it "Covers the whole project". The organization should immediately close the project and start again with a more qualified project manager.

If the company was to allow the project to proceed, as many unfortunately do, they will find that because there are no instructions on the contingency, it may be used inappropriately and out of proportion to cover poor project management. Many organizations have battle scars from such amateur decisions, and the author includes himself in that group. Project management orthodoxy also includes a management contingency for unforeseen risks. The author avoids this and puts more emphasis on quality project managers foreseeing and planning risks. This is necessary to bring the most accountability to the project management team and increase the accuracy of cost estimates.

Risks

This phase of project management planning is performed before the budget is complete. The end result of this risk planning, the cost of contingency, was applied to the budget in the above section. Risk planning is a very important section of all operations in general and project management in particular. We will not travel too deep in this book, but the author encourages further study of risk for all business owners and organization managers. The below text will examine the importance of identifying, categorizing, and prioritizing risks. Finally, we will plan for risks with established risk responses before determining their costs for the budget.

Identifying and Categorizing Risks

Risks are important within project management. They are identified before the project gained approval to begin in the business case and again in the project charter. During planning, they are identified with greater accuracy. Identifying risks is never completed unilaterally. If you are a small businessperson planning a project, use other project participants to identify risks. If you are a sole proprietor without employees, talk with a stakeholder to establish what they consider major and minor risks to the project. For companies with a project management team, identifying risks should be fun, interactive, and inclusive of all team members and stakeholders.

The primary methods for collecting risks may include the following: brainstorming, stakeholder interviews, and SWOT analysis. These are established tools in solution-based management and each requires good facilitation to draw the most benefit. During brainstorming, the facilitator must establish that there are no bad and dumb ideas. There are two great variations of getting these ideas on paper: shout them out to a facilitator who writes them down or the silent brainstorm that is compiled after an established period of time. The weakness of the shout out brainstorm is that quiet team members will invariably speak and shout less than the more outgoing members. And as the reader should know, a loud talkative personality does not equal correctness. For the silent brainstorm, each team member puts all of their ideas on a paper and those pieces of paper are then collected by the facilitator. The team, whether shouted or written, will then begin to categorize the risks and remove duplicates. This is a great start to risk management.

For stakeholder interviews, the facilitator schedules time with each stakeholder outside of the project team. It is important for the facilitator to not simply go to both customer and vendor, but also to the executive and middle managers of their own organization. This can be more time consuming and the facilitator may find that delegating team members to conduct some interviews is a best practice. Once the list of risks is compiled, the project manager may determine that some of the risks were previously identified. Great. The project manager may also find that a stakeholder identified some risks that are inapplicable. If the project manager finds that a risk is not a risk at all, she should document that and communicate this to both the stakeholder and project team. All risks, their responses, and potential costs should be documented in a risk register. This is a dynamic list that will be continuously updated until the close of the project and used as a benchmark for other similar future projects.

SWOT analysis, since its spread in the 20th century, has been a good tool to organize strengths, weaknesses, opportunities, and threats to a company or project. This chapter will not dissect this intuitive tool in detail. However, for risk analysis, focus on threats to both the project and company.

Prioritizing Risks

Throughout the life of the project, risks must be identified, assessed, and controlled. We assess risks by prioritizing their impact and probability. Impact is the effect of the risk on the project's benefit, costs, schedule, or scope. Establishing both impact and probability is subjective and can be hampered by individual bias and personal risk thresholds. The collective method to problem solving fences much of this away. However, project managers should encourage researched input and not simply opinions. Subject matter experts are great inputs while prioritizing risks. The project team should also have a numeric system for evaluating both impact and probability.

As an example, the system could rate both impact and probability from 1 – 5, with 5 being the most severe impact and the most likely to occur. A power grid outage may have an impact of 3 with a probability of 1. This, 3 X 1, would give this risk a value of 3. Catastrophic damage to a critical earth moving machine might have a 5 impact and a 2 probability, giving the risk a 10 value. The project team should have an established cutoff for risk priority values. In the above project, the cutoff is 6. Therefore, the team would prioritize responding to the backhoe ahead of the power outage. The team, through research and collective reasoning, will establish the cost to respond to the risk. Risks with a value equal to or less than 5 would be put on a watch list. The team does not need to actively plan resources to respond to them but it needs to stay abreast of their development. The cost, again, will fall off and be irretrievable after that activity has been completed and closed.

A note should be made for who is responsible for each risk response. Risk responses are both project and activity directed. The project directed risks are managed by the project manager. Activity risks should be managed by whichever team member is responsible for delivering the activity. In simple projects, the project manager may lead all activities. This is possible and favorable when the network diagram is streamlined, node after node within a finish to start relationship. However, on large or complex projects with multiple activities in progress simultaneously, team leaders and associate project managers take responsibility of the activity. This responsibility includes scope, schedule, costs, and risks. However, no team member is left alone. Project meetings are mandatory and the first order of business is risks. Team leaders of current activities will address and provide updates for the risks that were identified for that activity. Though responsible for the risk, the team member will receive ample input from other team members.

Risk Response

There are several established risk responses that project managers use to manage risks. Risk responses include avoid, mitigate, transfer, share, exploit, and enhance. It is natural for the reader to view risks as negative. However, in project management risks are events that could happen. Therefore, a known risk highlights uncertainly within the project. Risks are then grouped into either positive opportunities or negative threats. The above risk responses should be first selected to match the effects of the risk. The second selection factor for responses is cost effectiveness. The project manager wants to keep costs from ballooning and causing further risk within the project. The risk responses are grouped and detailed below.

Risk Responses for Negative Threats. Avoid, mitigate, and transfer are risk responses used for negative threats looming and lurking within projects. Avoiding a risk is not simply side stepping it. This response forces the project team to find the root cause of the risk and eliminate it before the risk arises. For a project that relies on a database for dynamic data, the risk of the database being attacked by a virus would present itself as a serious threat to the project. The solution may be to avoid this by creating a redundant database system. Mitigating a risk reduces the effect of the risk on the project by either reducing its probability, its impact, or both. For a construction project, a detailed training schedule for all employees is a great way to mitigate the risk of recurring personnel injury and equipment failures. Transferring a risk is a common approach to risk management. Risk transfer is seen when a company insures equipment and accidents. The project management team must select the most appropriate response with attention to the cost of implementation.

Risk Reponses for Positive Opportunities. Exploit, enhance, and share are risk responses for the positive opportunities that project managers should welcome. There is a fourth response for positive risks included by project management orthodoxy: reject. It was not covered because it is intuitive and rejection is hardly a response. Yet it is good for project managers and business owners to understand that opportunities do not need to be absorbed. Project management teams exploit opportunities by ensuring that the opportunity occurs. If there is a contractual incentive for an earlier delivery of the product to the customer, the project manager would exploit that by safely and professionally speeding up the project to earn that incentive. Enhancing an opportunity involves increasing either the probability, impact, or both of the risk occurring. The above opportunity of securing the early finish incentive will also be enhanced by training construction teams on standard operating procedures and having a benchmarking time on all job tasks. Both the exploiting and enhancing of this risk are accompanied by costs. The cost of additional resources to finish early and the training to tighten operations. These costs are fine as long as they do not exceed the incentive bonus.

The last risk response for opportunities is sharing. Sharing involves partnerships with other business owners and corporations. This is vital for small business practitioners and, unfortunately, does not happen enough. Sole proprietors, small companies, and medium enterprises would benefit greatly by teaming up to tackle larger projects. An example of this would be an engineering consulting firm contracted to solve civil engineering concerns. That same consulting firm may identify a need to modify the database. If the company agrees, that consulting firm could create a partnership or joint venture with an IT solutions firm to meet that opportunity. Though negative risks get more attention, project managers and business owners should look for positive opportunities within projects.

Again, the collective costs of risk responses are bundled as the contingency within the budget. The other element of the budget is the planned costs of each activity. Remember to collectively plan and account for risks.

Execution and Quality

It may appear that much of the work of projects is in planning. However, planning should be neither overly time consuming nor the bulk of the schedule. With our justification from the business case and our charter that provided approval, the project management team planned out scope, schedule, cost, and risks. It is now time to work and complete the project. Execution and quality are intertwined and this text joins their processes in an attempt to communicate their shared importance.

Project Work

The work to be completed does not need to be reorganized or dissected at this point in the project. The goal now is to follow the plan, measure quality, and communicate effectively. An important element of communication is the frequent project meeting. As stated earlier in the text, the first discussion of the meeting should be current risks to the activities in progress. This will determine the reaction of the team to the risk, through risk responses, if necessary and as predetermined. The flow of the project should be as seamless as possible and business leaders and project managers ensure this with positive communications to stakeholders.

Each activity produces a required segment of the project deliverable. There are three primary quality checks that must happen for the project manager, accidental or licensed, to be worth her weight in copper. The first is the internal check. This is performed while the work is being completed by a designated member of the team usually committed to quality throughout the project. This team member uses the established scope of the project and statistical modeling to determine if the project management team is heading in the right direction. Much of the defects, which is variance away from the scope, should be identified during these checks. Any defect will cause rework to correct the issue. Rework may have a negative effect on time, cash, and morale. Therefore, it is especially important to find defects as early as possible during this check. If a defect is undetected, it will usually be identified in the next quality check performed by the customer.

The second quality check is the customer check. When you acquire a product, you check that you are getting what you purchased. The quality of this check usually increases with the cost of the product. If a customer buys a turtleneck sweater that claims to be 100% cotton, he will usually believe the retailer and not take the $30 piece of clothing to a laboratory to have the material verified. However, if that same customer purchases a high definition smart television for $1,500, he will check every claimed function uttered by the electronics salesperson. The customer check on a project works in a similar way. After the internal check, the project manager presents the activity deliverable to the customer for formal acceptance. The customer either accepts or rejects. If the customer rejects, rework begins. The project manager must be certain that the deliverable is actually outside of scope. Customers attempting to add additional requirements have to be rejected as scope creep. Of course, ideas and plans change. If a customer wants something that is comparable, good practice is to make the change if it does not cause an increase in time and cost and does not expand the scope. However, if it does expand the scope, scope creep, the answer may not be to reject. Some organizations take that time to modify the offer. In short, anything is possible with the right budget.

The project manager check is the third and last check and is more of a project overwatch. Whereas the first and second checks are deliverable, and thus activity facing, this check takes a global view of the entire project. The emphasis here is that project performance is correctly aligned with the scope. This is an important step and should not be neglected.

Quality management through this three-check process produces projects that finish timely with limited amounts of rework. A project without quality checks is a disaster in the making. People, many times, choose the easier route to a destination. In this pursuit of comfort, people may begin removing otherwise needed processes. It would be a mistake for an organization to remove quality checks from a project. The amount of rework could be discouraging when the customer rejects all of the deliverables. To ensure the integrity of the project and the sanity of the project team, use these three checks to verify quality.

Close Activity and Project

This is a simple process. The activity will close once the customer accepts the activity deliverable. The project will close once the customer accepts the project deliverable or the project closes prematurely. The project may be terminated for any number of reasons that simply remove the justification to move forward. Continuous justification is an important concept in project management. Without justification, the project manager must stop immediately.

Whether closing an activity or phase, the final documentation and commentary should be recorded for future similar projects. Project management can be complicated and its orthodoxy is expansive. Let this project management section spark your interest to dig deeper into this great and necessary field.

Conclusion

We have reached the end of the operations chapter; but a business owner should push against the end of business operations. When the company no longer has operations on the horizon, it has reached the end of its useful life. Operations is the center of what pulled business owners away from employment. It is the bright attention-grabbing Venus in the black potential filled solar system of our business ideas. Few, regardless of educational attainment and stated expertise, look forward to creating business plans with financials and creating job descriptions to attract the most desirable candidates. The young and old dream about operations, in retail, in textile, in manufacturing, in construction, in database development; operations, big and small, local and global. The reader of this text should make a commitment to continuously learn for benchmarking and developing their operations.

Marketing

Marketing is the important area of the company that communicates the function of a product or service with a potential customer for revenue. This is critical, and many great companies failed miserably because their motivated customers did not know they existed. Modern marketing is often more complex than a weekly advertisement in the local newspaper. Marketing is a researched commitment to reach a designated portion of the general, or global, population. That research will contribute to the development of both an internal and external analysis of what is currently possible and probable. As the marketing strategy is decided and implemented, the organization will measure the results. The ability to use primitive marketing strategies and expect grand results have diminished over time with an increasingly global marketspace. Marketing, similar to other business functions, is both art and science. Let us reexamine the now beloved graphic.

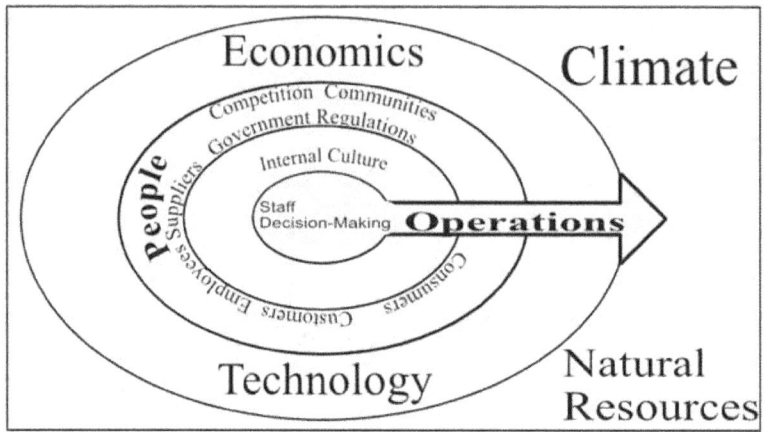

Marketing takes a comprehensive, though dynamic, view of both the external and internal environments. Therefore, all of the elements within this graphic are pertinent to marketing.

Market Research

Before much of the marketing decisions can be formed, research on the industry at large is required. Research, in its orthodoxy, begins with identifying the industry and its primary niches. This task appears both simple and static when it is actually dynamic and granular. The research should not end while your business is still operating. Small businessowners usually have a gritty tenacity to win. Tenacity may convert into driven obsession as the company becomes the life of the business owner. The idea of a respectable work life balance is discarded as short-term discomfort and long nights are traded for long-term success. Of course, research may not be the primary reason why the company lights burn late, but it is a contributing factor. This tenacity, or obsession, that researches, plans, performs, and measures can be a great advantage over rival companies.

Performing Research

Let us unpack the how of research. The most convenient resource for most individuals is the internet. Earlier in this text, we spoke of peer reviewed articles for human resources planning. That is not always the case with marketing research. You need to scour high and low to discover the competitors and trends of the industry. Another great marketing tool is past experience. It would be a bit naïve, for a businessowner to put a company in motion in an industry that they have yet to operate in any capacity. Most middle managers and entrepreneurs have both experience and contacts in the industry. A note should be made on franchising, which is an area of interest for many entrepreneurs. Many franchisees may not have experience in the industry; however, large franchises usually pride themselves on their training programs for new franchisees. Both, the franchisee entering into a training program and the independent entrepreneur with years of experience, reduce the research learning curve.

For the independent businessowner, contacts are great for research and securing contracts. Open conversations with industry practitioners and joining groups are great ways to stay ahead of the research curve. Real estate investors take advantage of pop up groups and other region-specific groups with likeminded individuals who attempt to break into the market using the latest skip tracing app. Professional groups, in project management and engineering detail the successes of others and give the details of how the project became possible, including pitfalls and workarounds. Unions are great for tradespeople. In unions, electricians and linemen can disgust the latest in safety and also upcoming contracts that qualified companies could exploit. For many small companies, the power of their network far exceeds that of their net worth.

Competitors

Research will organically create a list of competitors. A competitor is a business rival who a potential customer could choose over your company. Companies research rivals by retrieving and analyzing various data sets pertaining to size, contracts, product and service differentiation, and customer service. The manager then finds areas to exploit for a competitive advantage. A competitive advantage is a favorable position that an organization enjoys within its industry. As the reader has surely gathered, competitors come and go and this list will be very dynamic. Not only do rivals enter and leave the operational arena, there capacities and competencies may change dramatically in short notice. Stay informed.

Key Success Factors (KSFs)

This is a buzz word used in various industries. The biggest mistake that managers commit is the belief that they determine key success factors. KSFs are outputs of research. Thorough research will determine what is critical for success in the industry. Examples of KSFs may include strong customer service, reliable fulfillment processes with limited waste, strong product research and development, and access to capital. The KSFs of an industry must not be ignored.

Access to capital is a certain barrier to entry in many industries. Barriers to entry stop great ideas from flourishing at a responsible level. Access to capital is a basic, though still complex, issue for getting started with most business ideas. We covered this in the financial chapter. Imagine having great and progressive ideas for the management of an airline. Naturally, you thought that if you could manage an airliner, you would reduce global carbon emissions, increase customer satisfaction, and grow the profit margin. Unfortunately, the feet of the idea would hit gravel when you recognize that you do not have billions of dollars or a rich uncle to implement your idea. You could shift your idea from ownership to consulting to secure a contract. You could also climb the corporate ladder as a manager within an existing airline to share your ideas more organically. Therefore, because of the barrier to entry caused by the access to capital KSF, the idea of a startup, in this instance, is unrealistic.

With research completed and key success factors in hand, the manager is ready to move ahead to determining how the company fits into the industry through the lens of its strengths and weaknesses.

Strength Weakness Opportunity Trend Threat (SWOTT)

The modified SWOTT business tool is a common framework to list the landscape of the industry through the vantage point of the business. It is intuitive. It requires honesty. It can be both expansive and simple. The author has seen several business plans that are nothing more than an elaborate, and oftentimes verbose, SWOTT tool. Others are more concise, putting the tool on a chart and not allowing it to exceed a couple of pages.

Strengths

This is the fun part of the analysis. This is where we take a swing for the fences and exaggerate the state of our organization, right? No. Strengths should be an honest state of what your company is capable of doing today.

This is not a projection. Business owners and managers are not dreaming of a great horizon. They are unpacking what can now be done to add value to the company. These strengths are internal and come to life when put in line with key success factors. The manager must find and list the core competencies.

Competencies are assets bundled into organizational capabilities. The reader should keep this simple explanation in mind as we move through some definitions. Resources are assets separated by tangibility. This is often an orthodox definition of assets that groups technology, reputation, and human capital and ingenuity as intangible while trucks, buildings, and financial assets are determined to be tangible. The reader should understand that resources are assets that the company utilizes with an established plan. Therefore, a rug on the entrance floor is an asset but it is not a resource. The toilet and the sink, all assets, all had a cost and have a value, but they will be omitted when we collect inventory of company resources.

Capabilities highlights how the organization will exploit the resource. Once this framework is in place, the organization will find its core competencies. These are the coordination of capabilities. Core competencies are the collection of internal activities that are central to the company's behavior. These are necessary for understanding how your firm operates and to determine what exactly is possible. Gathering core competencies for a small or flat organization is usually straight forward. However, for large, multi-national firms splintered into departments and divisions, this core competencies will be gathered only after the competencies of each department is determined. Core competencies are collective in their nature and cannot be division specific. This will require a bit more work; yet, the manager within a large organization should appreciate the glut of tools within arm's reach.

With possibilities in hand in the form of core competencies, the manager must now look outward into the sea of rivals operating in the same industry and determine what are the organization's distinctive competencies. Distinctive competencies are activities that the company performs better than its competition. This is the true strength of the company. Yes, we list out the assets, resources, capabilities, and core competencies. The reason why that list comes about is to get to the distinctive competencies. These are the list of strengths that will put your rivals on their heels. This list of strengths, resource based at their core, will change dynamically. Core competencies will alter because of internal changes and distinctive competencies will change as rivals become stronger or weaker in comparison. It is possible, for a company to gain a distinctive competency with little effort as a competitor loses its edge. Managers should look to maintain the organization's current distinctive competencies while positioning the company to convert core competencies to distinctive ones as a dynamic list of strengths. The moment your organization loses its focus, another smarter more useful company will fill the void created by your absence.

For distinctive competencies to have lasting power as sustainable and profitable organizational strengths, they must be realistically repeatable. Distinctive competencies are not fleeting ideas. They are established plans for using resources comparatively better than the company's rivals. A patent is a great way to have a repeatable product that is durable. It is also a great way to ensure that rivals cannot easily encroach upon your product. As companies identify their distinctive competencies, they should also create a plan for sustaining that position.

Weaknesses

Your organization is air tight without even a dent in your armor. You are awesome, you, your friends, and your mother all agree on this observation. So, you skip this part of the SWOTT analysis. Or, even more deceptively, you give considerable time to this section and discover that you have no weaknesses to list. The demand is simple, if you do not have weaknesses you are not in business and you should start the internal investigative process over. Start the process over as many times as necessary to create a list of weaknesses.

A great way to identify weaknesses is to compare resource gaps between your company's current position and the key success factors for the industry. If the industry lists ecommerce as a KSF, you would be mistaken to check the box because you have a running website. A closer look may determine that your website is inadequate. Perhaps it is too cluttered, has poor updates, and experience technical difficulties too often. This would be a clear weakness that should be addressed. Another weakness may be the skills of the workforce and the gap between the outputs of those skills and the tools necessary to achieve success factors.

The weakness list is also dynamic as managers look to shorten it and as other weaknesses present themselves. Managers target this list by committing future investments to develop required resources. You cannot fix what you refuse to acknowledge, and that is why this list is important.

It is easy for companies to continue to invest in their strengths, and though strengths should not be left stagnant, it would be a mistake to ignore weaknesses and allow them to continuously fester until they founder the company.

Advisory Board

A note should be made to the importance of the advisory board for small companies. Larger corporations have internal systems in place to identify and list strengths and weaknesses dynamically. For small companies and startups, the ease of getting through this process can create unilateral decisions. This is especially true when the entrepreneur holds decades of experience in the industry. The idea that I know what I am doing, I understand the niche, I know my strengths, and I can manage to diminish the impact of my weaknesses, is a very hazardous line of thinking. That very know-it-all thinking increases the risk profile of the entire organization. The advisory board is a great solution to such absurd reasoning.

The advisory board can be made up of people, and perhaps machines, with or without experience in the industry. You would be surprised the amount of great ideas that someone could offer a new construction company without having ever spent a day holding a shovel or commanding an excavator. The reason this holds true is because many decisions are not industry specific. The idea of securing a loan to purchase equipment is not specific to the construction industry. For the other industry specific ideas, fresh eyes and thoughts is a huge advantage that breaks the mold of 'But this is how we have always done it'. That line, which is prevalent throughout humanity has been a wall to great ideas and a cliff for innovation. Dare to be different. Consider, with an advisory board, the methods that have not been utilized in your industry. Find a consensus with your advisory board on both the strengths and weaknesses of your company and the opportunities, threats, and trends of your industry.

Opportunities

Establishing realistic opportunities is usually the first step to planning how to answer the external environment. This suggested order is not an established rule. You can start with trends or threats. The reason why many managers prefer to begin with opportunities could be explained by their optimistic nature. Optimism could be defined as the resilient belief in an awesome future despite all negative factors. Blind optimism, though important to team morale, is baseless. Educated and insightful optimism is a great asset to an organization. The difference could be captured in the following two individuals. Bobbi is on a cruise ship in international waters. The ship is attacked by a missile from a foreign military that mistook the ship for a war vessel. While everyone is panicking, Bobbi is optimistic that things will work out. Bobbi's optimism is baseless and it is standing in the way of finding a solution to the problem at hand. In the second example, Toure is on a plane when it hits very rough turbulence. The flight attendant, unprepared for what lay ahead, is thrown to the ceiling of the plane along with her refreshment trolley. The flight attendant is knocked unconscious. A passenger screams in agony as the trolley fell upon him and broke his collar bone. The travelers not wearing seatbelts also hit the ceiling of the plane and now groan in misery. The flight teeters and dives. Passengers are screaming and crying and others are praying. Toure, understanding the statistical odds of a plane crashing because of turbulence, smiles and waves at a crying baby to ease the child's confusion. He cracks a joke with the lady sitting beside him. Eventually, enough travelers see Toure's demeanor and begin to relax and cool. Toure, having calmed down the passengers, could now administer aid to the injured individuals. Viewing opportunities through the lens of optimism and information is impactful.

Opportunities are dynamic targets that competencies can now exploit. Before the organization pins back its ears and runs toward an opportunity, it must determine the revenue potential of its competence. It must know how it will exploit that opportunity and what will it earn for its efforts. For example, a construction company determines that the request for proposal for a local library is an opportunity. It must now determine the revenue, and profit, of winning that contract. It must then, determine the opportunity cost of choosing a different project. The public library, may have a longer process time from proposal to contract. It may also require more time to earn the contract through presentations and interviews. The local library costs $1,000,000 (it is very small). Even though this is an opportunity that the construction company can exploit, resources are always limited and a decision must be made. The cost of doing business with a local municipality, with its red tape and redundancies, may prove less appetizing in comparison to smaller faster contracts. The company refuses to submit a proposal. Onlookers may see this as leaving a million dollars on the table, but the company planned and understood that they will earn that money in half the time with a fraction of the headaches. Though a company identifies an opportunity, it may also choose to ignore it.

Trends

Trends are identified by consistent research. They can become either opportunities or threats of various magnitudes. Staff should look not only to identify these trends but also determine their impact on operations and the best way to either accept and exploit or avoid and mitigate these trends. A common example of a positive trend is the development of the area of operation with either private or public funds. This is a trend that usually lasts years; hopefully without an end in sight. An owner of an apartment building with 30 units should be excited that three new restaurants are opening and that a large government building is under construction in the area. This excitement will only increase as the presence of young vibrant professionals trends higher. These trends in local development and population will allow the apartment building owner to charge more for rent, thus improving her bottom line.

An example of a negative trend is the use and prevalence of tax preparation websites and software in the United States. This is negative for many accountants who earn much of their revenue during the tax season. An accountant who noticed this trend, hopefully several years ago, would need to make serious decisions to protect the revenue of his business. Perhaps he would focus more on corporate taxes. Perhaps he would close his business and get a job in a corporation. The decision that this accountant would make should be guided by research and presented to his organization's established advisory board. Whatever decision is made, companies must identify and prepare for trends affecting their industries.

Threats

Threats are the opposite of opportunities and are the negative risks that the organization highlights in its current environment or within its planning horizon. Similar with weaknesses, threats are usually skipped around by managers and businessowners. Yet, every industry has threats that present themselves to different companies operating in the same space. Therefore, if the reader cannot find threats than the reader cannot find honesty. A blank page is either the effect of dishonesty or poor research. Both will poison the company in the near future. There are few things that hurt companies as much as a threat rolling down the train track only to hit an organization that refused to face reality.

Threats are the equivalent of negative risks covered early in this text. As with project risks, the organization must determine how best to answer the challenge of the threat. Sometimes the threat is so certain and so impactful that the best course of action is to get out of the industry while you still have a profit. This is usually not the case; however, each threat must be evaluated and planned with intellect over emotion. Threats and risks hold similar categories of responses: mitigate and avoid.

A major threat in a global market, is the rising cost of inputs. A company that operates with a multinational supply chain is potentially affected by political insecurities and increased costs at home and abroad. A company creating sustainable rubber shoes with synthetic material, sourcing its rubber from Brazil and its recycled synthetic material locally has known and unknown threats. Wildfires in Brazil is a direct threat to the source of inputs that will potentially raise the cost of rubber. The protests to Brazil's response to the wildfires may threaten the safety and timeliness of transportation within the supply chain. This delay, caused by insecurity at Brazilian ports will increase the fulfillment times and potentially reduce customer service and brand loyalty, thus creating another threat.

The threat of increased cost of rubber could be mitigated by creating and signing a contract with your vendor that locks the cost of rubber for a specified duration of time. Of course, cost increases are usually for legitimate reason and not to hobble your company; therefore, strong negotiation skills will be handy here. This threat could also be avoided by having several options for vendors used concurrently. Concurrent vendors, greatly reduces the risk of stalled operations because of a risk becoming reality. If the Brazilian rubber vendor increases the cost of rubber by 35% because of political unrest, the Guatemalan producer may not only have a stable cost, but might lower the cost per pound as the size of your purchase increases. The idea of threats is to identify them before creating plans to mitigate or avoid the risk.

There are two other important threats that each organization should consider: new rivals and substitutes. This was covered in the section on strengths when admonishing managers to find distinctive competencies and continue the pressure on rivals less that advantage be lost. Of course, this risk is not a strength, it is an ordinary threat that should be expected by any operating company. Companies compete for position from approaching competitors and lurking substitutes by competing on price. More established companies may have better and more seasoned supply chains and processes that allow for lower prices for customers. Brand loyalty, a major goal of marketing is also achieved by successfully fulfilling customer orders over time. This brand loyalty keeps customers from rivals and substitutes. Quality managers understand that their work, is never complete. They may take a vacation or a sick day, but the organization's competitors is always peering over the fence to secure a stronger position. Processes for marketing and positioning core competencies are the winning recipe over superstar managers. In most organizations, managers come and go; yet, the hope of the company is that it endures numerous business cycles through successful planning and action.

The SWOTT analysis is a common tool in its use around the world. It has been used with brevity and expanded to cover the entire plan with success. This text hopes to convey that one tool should not replace a toolbox. Learn as much as possible – while operating your company. The notion of analysis paralysis, a state of consistent learning about outcomes that substitutes action, is not an issue for determined managers. Quality staff understand that plans are necessary, and equally important are the measures of past performance. SWOTT, requiring honesty to unlock its potential, highlights both the internal and external environments. This environmental scanning gives further insight on the organizational aspirations held by both managers and businessowners. There are other tools that may substitute the SWOTT analysis. These tools include the PESTE analysis, which lists political, economic, sociocultural, technical, and environmental factors that affect the possibilities of operations. Whichever tool the organization uses, the focus remains the same: give the company the best chance of success considering its industrial environment.

Marketing Strategies

Marketing, like so many business functions, is filled with tons of jargon. The military is filled with acronyms and jargon. Veterans are often told to reduce their use as they prepare to leave the army and enter the general population. Project management is littered with industry talk that acts like a barrier to entry for the neophyte. The best project managers can explain, in a single brief meeting, any process to both the project management office (PMO) and a stakeholder from a local community organization. Information technology is arguably the king of jargon. Some IT professionals are guilty of enjoying the cringe that they see on the faces of managers and users when explaining an element of a database or application. These professionals throw jargon words to self-aggrandize and stop the exchange from escalating into an educational conversation. Marketing has not escaped this criticism. However, this book looks to be the bulb in the tunnel for the beginning business practitioner while also sharpening the experienced manager. This book is not a jargon encyclopedia, though we admittedly use a few. This book was written with the score in mind; to use a sports analogy. The purpose of this chapter is to build the foundational structure of marketing for enterprise. The prior section explaining the why and how of marketing research. This section will examine marketing strategies that put the company in a favorable position to increase revenue.

Brand Loyalty

A common goal of marketing is brand recognition. However, it is not enough for customers to know that your brand and product exists. It is not enough for the average homeowner to understand that your company gives

X amount of scholarship to kids in need and provides X amount of food trucks to hungry families during Thanksgiving. Both the initiatives and the marketing to get the story told are great. All fantastic. However, if your company is for profit, it is revenue that matters most. For non-profit organizations, it is donations that keep many of them afloat over government grants. So, for both the non-profit organization and the for-profit company, it is the choice of individuals to either purchase a good or service or provide a donation for a worthy cause. This is captured in the Awareness, Interest, Desire, and Action (AIDA) acronym.

Awareness and interest are recognition. Desire and Action are success. Action is the purchase of a good or service. The last two steps of AIDA in repetition is brand loyalty. The heart of brand loyalty is not simply creative marketing. The secret of brand loyalty is not how many commercials the organization launches during the most watched television programs. The secret to brand loyalty is not much of a secret at all. Have a great product and the customers who find it will not forget it. Simple.

A great example of this is diet sodas. In the 1950s and 1960s, several soda brands experimented with diet beverages. United States was becoming more health conscious and the target market was slightly older and rounder than that of regular sodas. Yes, these companies poured millions into marketing. Yet, that did not bring them ultimate success. Success came primarily because it was a product that did not sacrifice taste for a slimmer waistline. It was a great product. The marketing of a great product is exponentially easier than the marketing of a failure. It was also found that the margins of diet soda were much more favorable than regular soda. The second highest cost of soda is sugar. With that cost removed, the potential for massive growth was intensified. This is the perfect storm for a company: a new product with a more appealing profit margin that potential customers love. This is the best route for marketing, not to make something from nothing but instead to bring great products and services to the forefront.

Growth Opportunities

Companies, as in the above soda example, should look to grow. There are four primary areas for growth opportunities: market penetration, market development, product development, and diversification.

Market Penetration

Companies penetrate a market when they use a current product or service to further dominate the market. This should occur naturally for companies that enjoy a distinctive competency. Push the product harder and encroach upon the audience and customers of the competition. If you are offering diet soda, and there are four primary competitors to your brand, you must first understand the connection that the competition has with their customers. These customers may identify with a marketing strategy that gears towards a younger audience. To enter into this rival's market share, your organization would need to determine the best communicate to reach this young audience. This is a great strategy to grow the company.

Market Development

Market development is a growth strategy that places a current product or service into a new market. Organization's that use this strategy find new places to sell their product, either geographically or in a near symmetrical industry where the benefits of the offering can be exploited. A different geographical location is intuitive; yet, new market research is still vital. Rugged hiking boots with great revenue in the United States may do well in Botswana with its high outback tourism industry. However, those same boots may do poorly in Saudi Arabia as that country appreciates a different level of outdoor activity. An unplanned decision is the surest way to founder a company. A near symmetrical industry is one where an offering can provide benefits to a new market's customer or consumer. A company cutting and supplying wood planks to a construction company may find that a public utilities organization requires the same planks for shoring field trenches. The company, using the same planks, found a new market to penetrate. Market development is a great way to expand the company beyond what was originally thought possible.

Product Development

Product development is a strategy that introduces another product into the same operating market. This strategy looks to build on the brand recognition of the company by deploying a new offering after research and development. Research and Development (R&D), should be a natural and ongoing process in all organizations to promote continuous improvement. As we established earlier, research is the basis of competition. Research allows managers to best steer operations into positive trends and opportunities while avoiding and mitigating threats and negative trends. R&D is important in both product development and diversification. During the product development growth opportunity, a soda company may introduce a new flavor. In this example, research has identified opportunities with orange flavored sodas. This segment of the larger soda industry has exploded in recent months and the company wants to capture additional market share by introducing this product. To capture that share, the company researches the niche before developing the product within a justifiable project. The finished product is then marketed to the audience identified as having an affinity for orange flavored sodas.

Diversification

Companies that diversify develop a new product for a new industry. Brand recognition may follow the company into the new industry. Experience is a barrier to entry that is tackled through strong research and development processes. If R&D is not a highlighted strength of a company, its lack of preparation and its ability to complete a project may not only add risk and reduce the chances of diversification being a success but it may also destroy the entire company. Diversification is the riskiest of all growth opportunities and it requires a stable and mature research and development department.

Avenues of Communication

There are several methods for passing a message to the potential customer. Before this text goes over these methods, it is important that we highlight the value of creativity. So much of marketing is captured in the magic of creativity. These marketing methods can be combined or thrown to the wayside. Research, which led this chapter, should provide insight on the best strategy for reaching your audience. Obviously, large organizations with a larger budget for marketing will have teams dedicated to reaching their target. These teams will use data with creativity to author the sometimes bizarre television commercials and signage lining expressways. These teams will usually mix the methods of communication into one of the following: radio and television advertisement and internet marketing.

Of course, there are many more strategies such as direct selling where salespeople knock on doors at odd hours and attempt to convince you to purchase the single greatest vacuum cleaner. Another strategy that will not be covered in detail in this text is telemarketing. Most readers are familiar with the unsolicited calls from telemarketers. These salespeople span nearly every industry, and the sophisticated telemarketers have data that led them to the potential customer. They call about everything from health care insurance to vehicle purchases, and some telemarketers such as real estate wholesalers may call to purchase the very house in which you are residing. This text does not cover these methods, and groups them separate from advertisement and web marketing, because they are deeply irritating to the targeted audience. Marketing should be a win-win situation for both the company and the customer. It is not a tricky word-game. It is not refusing to take no for an answer. That is bullying and very disturbing for many potential customers. Instead of trying to push a product or service down the throat of a retired grandma, it is best to find the demographic that matches the offering.

In the above text, we considered companies large enough to have dedicated marketing personnel and teams. We must also give attention to the small company and the sole practitioner. These organizations must use more creativity to reach a target audience and more energy to wear multiple hats. Creativity shines in the face of limited resources. A small company could only dream of a National Football League Superbowl commercial. That small company with those awesome products could change the trajectory of its business life with such an advertisement. However, that small company and that sole practitioner cannot afford that marketing. Therefore, local advertisements and internet marketing are a great, and realistic, way to communicate the benefits of your offerings.

Co-Branding

With radio and television marketing, there are tons of books and consultants that can give you the details of how to construct an awesome advertisement. This text highlights this strategy for a different reason: co-branding. Co-branding is the art of combining two or more companies into a single advertisement. It is an art because it must be brought together delicately. It is important enough to find its way into this text because not enough small companies co-brand. Co-branding is mostly seen on the larger national stage. Perhaps you have viewed an advertisement of a movie and a popular soda beverage. Then again maybe you saw an advertisement of a basketball team that stated if the team reaches 100 points, you can take your ticket to a fast food restaurant and pick up a free taco or burger. This is co-branding and it is highly effective. Small companies should not miss the opportunity to work together in advertisement.

When organizations search for companies to co-brand with, they must ensure both companies hold equal positions in brand awareness, reputation, and logically fit together. The logical fit, can be immediately drawn in the previous examples of co-branding: movie and basketball. In the basketball example, food and sports are compliments to one another. Some homes have a tradition of watching a game from the comfort of their home with platters of food before them. In the movie example, it is again a compliment, soda, that allows for the two companies to work together. This fit, many times based on culture, allows the companies to maximize the benefits of the marketing strategy while minimizing its disadvantages.

When co-branding, the reputation of the other company is of great importance. It would do massive harm to have advertisement with a company in the fog of scandal. For example, a smartphone organization considers co-branding with a bank marketing its mobile banking features. The bank recently had a massive breach of its database that put the personal information of over a million customers at risk. If the smartphone organization co-brands with this bank, it may, by law of proximity, appear unsecure and risky. In fact, this partnership could cause serious image and brand loyalty damage. In this scenario, it would be best for the smartphone company to decline this partnership in protection of its reputation.

Brand awareness is another important factor when co-branding. One company should not carry the other. For each company to absorb the maximum benefits, they must hold an equal stature. They must have, separately, brand equity. If Company O is a national brand and Company Z is a regional brand, this marketing strategy would unjustly benefit Company Z. Brand equity is the action, or revenue, section of brand awareness. In the above example, the scope of Company O's equity far exceeds that of Company Z. This produces an illogical fit and should be avoided. Co-branding is not charity. It is the idea that two companies of equal positions in their respective industries can work together to achieve a stated goal.

Measuring Marketing

Smart businesses measure their decision making. Terrible decisions abound in the business world. If any leader claims that they have a spotless record of awesome decisions, just walk away. They are not including honesty into the conversation. Some decisions may be justified at the roundtable but fail in the field. Some decisions are obvious, such as co-branding, during the start only to fall apart as an external input enters into the partnership. Measuring matters. It is part of the idea of control and quality assurance. If an idea is not working, it is aborted. This is a similar idea found in the above project management section of the operations chapter. The idea that justification is continuously sought throughout the life of the project or marketing strategy is vital for reputation, brand equity, and resources. Companies are always admonished to not throw cash down the catch basin and control their communication.

Measuring in Practice

For sophisticated organizations, measuring decisions in quantitative terms is a business analyst function. Dedicated information technology staff look at decisions through the lens of several metrics. Large and medium companies are increasingly appreciating the importance of business intelligence staff. These analysts, and sometimes data scientist, will determine if the metrics were met, and company leadership will guide their searches and queries through databases. Some data scientists and analysts will take early data and predict future outcomes through modeling. For small organizations who have yet to budget an analyst's services, the work comes down to managers. They wear multiple hats. The Marketing Manager may also be the Finance Manager. The Chief Operating Officer may also be the Project Manager and the Lead Analyst. When you are small, not having the budget to get the staff of your dreams is not an excuse. You do what you must until you can do it better.

In the above scenario, the Chief Operating Officer (COO) measures the work of the Marketing Manager. They are small but they managed to set up a free database. They manually entered in all the appropriate data to avoid the Garbage In Garbage Out (GIGO) theory. They determine that the co-branding worked well. They measured Leads per strategy, sales per lead, and profit per sale. The COO recognizes that there are numerous other queries that he can search; but, the organization has agreed that this is a great place to begin.

Decision measurement requires a quantitative base to measure against. How do we know if 10 people purchasing per minute between 8:00pm and 9:00pm represents an increase unless we know what it was before the strategy was deployed? With the pre-strategy data in hand, the COO measures leads per strategy. He finds that after the co-branding, the amount of traffic to the website increased by 150%, from 500 average unique visitors in a day to 1250. The COO remembered the important of data visualization and created a graphic to express this to the organization. He sent the below by email.

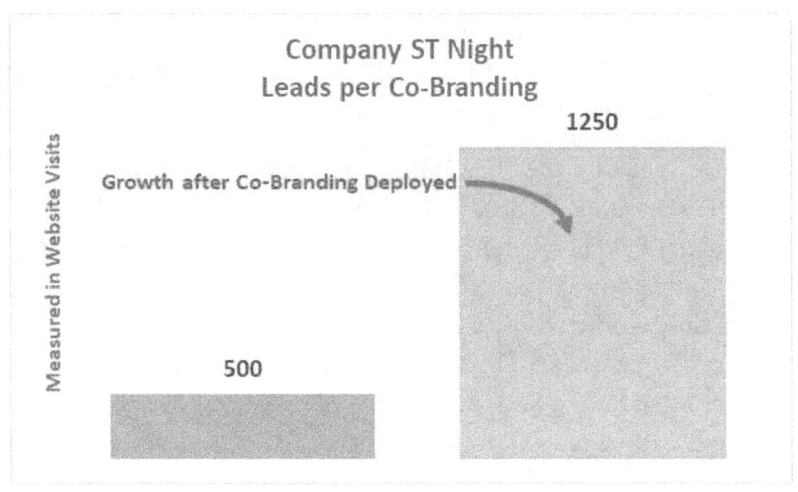

The COO gets the attention of the team and the organization understands that it is not bias because Marketing Manager did not perform the analysis. He now analyzes the revenue per lead. This is basic arithmetic when the correct data has been entered into the database. He gets to work. The below graphic shows, as he explains in an email, the amount of sales per daily leads. We have seen the daily website visitors, leads, increase from 500 to 1250 in Graphic 5.2. The amount of leads converted into purchases increased from 7% to 15%. The average cost of products remained the same at $15. The results show a successful marketing strategy, as daily revenue increased from over $500 to nearly $3000.

Finally, the COO wants to look at the profitability of that increased revenue. Big revenue is better than small revenue even if profit margin, as a percentage, is smaller. The COO works with the Marketing Manager to determine the full cost of the co-branding. He has the number, and instead of creating another graphic, he sends an email that details what needs to happen for the company to breakeven. This could take the form of a breakeven analysis if a graphic is preferred. The Marketing Manager, working as the Finance Manager, now works with the COO for this breakdown. They determine, together, that it would take approximately 55 days to breakeven from the co-branding expenditures. That is great, as the co-branding effects will last long after those 55 days. The organization, now filled with quantifiable knowledge of the variance, can state with confidence that the co-branding strategy was a success.

Conclusion

Marketing is an important aspect of business. Operations should look to create awesome products and services that benefit customers. It is the task of marketing departments, divisions, and sole practitioners to communicate that benefit. For many startups, small companies, and sole practitioners, the cost of a dedicated marketing position may not be practical. The necessity of marketing does not waiver based on the available budget of the organization. Be creative.

SWOTT is an important tool for marketing. It is a great foundational tool for research. The strengths of an organization will determine which opportunities it strives for and how it strategizes capturing a target audience. Trends, categorized as either negative or positive, are won by companies that have a strong research and development culture. Without constant research, an organization is purely a reactor. It is in continuous reaction mode. Though this company may slip and fall into a measure of success, it will be fleeting. Smart companies know the importance of understanding the industry's horizon and plan accordingly.

The idea of co-branding was covered in great detail in this chapter. The author wishes to encourage small companies and sole practitioners to work together on as many marketing projects as possible. Small companies, with limited resources, should pull back the layers of distrust and find more eager entrepreneurs of products and services that compliment your own. This is a great strategy for cutting cost, reaching a demographic that your company had yet to consider, and expanding the possibilities of tomorrow. Measure success and duplicate it to doubling affects again and again.

Success In Practice

Success is a journey on a dimly lit path. The path looks different to different people. One business owner starts down their journey to free themselves from the carousel of seemingly sadistic bosses that litter corporate offices. Another finds business as a necessity to increase their income. Perhaps this second entrepreneur begins with a 'hustle' before organizing this side gig into a respectable company. Regardless of how the entrepreneur found the path, all have an idea of how best to bring value to potential customers. Or at least all should after reading this book.

Dr. Neil deGrasse Tyson, an astrophysicist not normally quoted in books on organizational success, states that people make money when other people understand how to make money from your offering. This is true for both the employee and the entrepreneur. Certainly, the business owner keeps an eye on their offering more than the employee keeps focus on their skill level. The employee, usually huddled in both comfort and fear, may never find the courage to write that book or start that company. The business owner differs from the average employee, not because she does not feel the emotion of fear in the face of uncertainty. She differs because she willingly steps into her fear and exploits opportunity with a quality plan for her offerings.

Fear and Worry

However, fear is a persistent internal threat for individuals throughout the world. It is the primary roadblock keeping wonderful and shockingly talented people from unveiling themselves to a receptive world. What if my book fails? What if I leave my position and my business falters? Should I co-found a start up with a friend when I have a comfortable position and a large office? Your mind, safety hugging and risk averse by its nature, will try to abort most ideas. The reader may find procrastination setting in, with the reading of book after book on general motivation. All of this could be described as a level of nervousness that Dr. Claire Weeks addresses expertly in her book 'Hope And Help For Your Nerves'.

Dr. Claire Weeks

In the aforementioned book, Dr. Weeks prescribes three awesome steps to getting out of your own way and pushing past nervousness and anxiety: face the anxiety, accept that it is there, and float past it. It is not quite enough to know that you are nervous about putting a company into motion. Is it the idea that the customers will not arrive and purchase your goods and services? Is it the belief that you cannot secure the appropriate financing to scale the business in a meaningful and sustainable way? Or is it the idea that you may have to work harder and longer than you have before? Whatever the reasons for your nervousness, it is great when the budding businessperson gets them down on paper.

Budding businesspersons is a term used to highlight the initial nervous state that appears when forming a business. This person at that time can find plenty of motivation from books and inspirational videos. There are several gurus that attempt to give these entrepreneurs a kick in the pants. These self-help gurus have found great success with programs and books that usually provide very little on the 'how' side of business. This book is not a motivational program. The reader should find motivation, organically, as she learns the facets of business operations and understands that high performance is in her grasp. An entrepreneur, with plans in hand and approaching the first step of operations, should rest assured that it is his behavior that makes the difference. In this way, it is knowledge (not overeducation) that assists in quieting the voices of dissent. Overeducation is highlighted here as there is a fine line between "One more book before I start" and one more month of procrastination.

Dr. Weeks writes that the next step in getting past our fears is to accept that they are present. We have listed them, as erroneous and off-topic as they may appear. Next, we must accept that they are present. This is a great time to add someone else into your internal conversation and make an affinity chart to best categorize these fears. Once they are grouped, begin to find sensible and realistic solutions. Your partner should help keep the list from growing exponentially in an attempt to further stall the business idea. If the fears are legitimate risks, and if you cannot realistically avoid or mitigate those risks, then the idea may need to be halted. However, if you are at this stage of planning, the risks were considered weeks ago. Be confident and allow your partner to help guide the session.

Eventually, the entrepreneur will arrive at her path for a jog into greatness. The reader must understand that some fears may linger. Dr. Claire Weeks describes this moment as floating past nervousness. The anxiety is there, we jotted it down and analyzed it. However, we do not wait for all fears to slide down a manhole before we move forward. We trust our planning and our abilities and take whatever fears remain on a joyride to success.

Operations Focused Leadership

Business functions orbit around the gravitational pull of operations. In all of your successes and gains, it is important for leaders to remember that business operations dynamically rest behind all decisions. Our favorite chart is below.

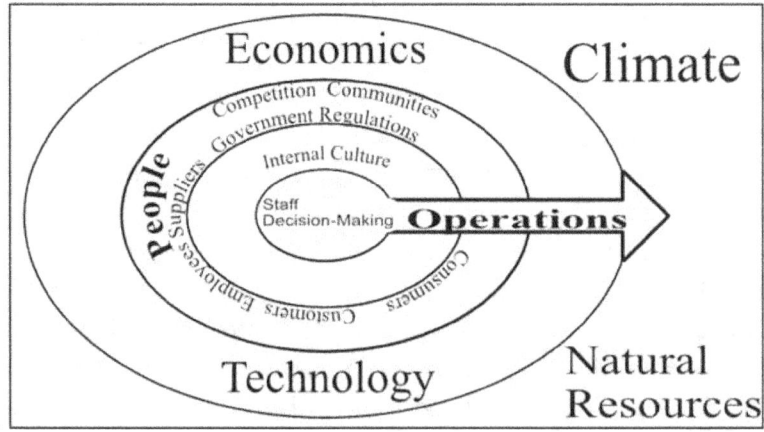

In the above chart, each of the factors within different spheres of influence ask questions. They make statements. Some make demands. Each question should be answered through the perspective of healthy operations. Each statement should be considered in light of relevant operations. Each demand should receive a response from the position of strong operations. This idea is the center of this book.

Operations Focused Army

The United States Army, with its critical international missions, trains its Soldiers to think of operations first. The Army captures this idea in the Warrior Ethos. This ethos statement is direct and places missions within the first sentence: 'I will always place the mission first'. The second and third sentences are: 'I will never accept defeat, I will never quit'. The second and third sentences support the first. Soldiers are admonished to not accept defeat when reaching for the mission (operations) and never quit in their pursuits. It is only after those sentences surrounding operations that we find the last sentence of the Warrior Ethos: 'I will never leave a fallen comrade.' Many organization leaders look to military leaders and warriors for answers on how best to approach business decisions. Managers and entrepreneurs read books like The Art of War by Sun Tzu for solutions to unique issues. The United States Army gives a concise clue in a single mantra repeated and memorized by teenagers in training. Operations are first. They are above all else. They are the reason why we are here. Without focused operations, employees wander directionless.

General Paik Sun Yup

General Paik Sun Yup, South Korea's first Four-Star Army General, puts this mission first belief into words in his book 'From Pusan to Panmunjom'. Gen. Paik, the highest ranking South Korean Officer during the Korean War, describes being surrounded by the Chinese Army. His division advanced into an ambush. It was the idea of keeping operations first that allowed his division to fight for days in a bloody battle instead of surrendering to a numerically superior enemy. Gen Paik understood that their mission of a free South Korea was more important than the individual lives of his troops. Entrepreneurs are encouraged to always perceive the external environment through the lens of business operations.

The above example of an ambushed Gen Paik also draws in the idea of walking forward in fear. It is the second lesson that troops can teach the business community. Certainly, there are troops who lost their ability to fear through repetition and supreme dedication. Yet, many other troops serve honorably despite fear. Readers should remember that it is how you behave in the face of fear that will determine the success of your company.

Business Plan

The business plan is required by nearly all investors and banks when attempting to secure the necessary capital to move a business forward. Though companies use or update these documents for external cash, managers are encouraged to make a practice of forming and updating business plans for internal use. The business plan is a guide and managers of all levels and of varying tenure can benefit from this document. We will sum up this document below. The reader should remember that the goal is not to create 70 pages of fluff. Managers should not attempt to make the heaviest firewood replacement possible. Business plans should be concise and focused. Any serious investor that is considering purchasing shares of your organization will ask for specific information that is not in the plan. As an example, if your plan has a 36-month cash flow projection, and an investor wants a 60-month projection, you will simply extend it and send it over. Banks usually have checklists for business loans that keep entrepreneurs on track. The below elements of a business plan are not only necessary for external stakeholders but also for the strategic management of your company.

If there is any portion of the below that seems a bit hazy, refer back to the section of this text and reread. When developing a business plan, follow the below outline and adjust where necessary:

1. Strategic Information (Chapter 1)

    a. Who are you? State your mission and vision statements.

    b. What are you reaching for? State your strategic objectives.

    c. State your strategy to secure your objectives. This is your product or service.

2. Resources (Chapter 2)

    a. How many people are currently employed?

    b. How many are needed to accomplish your strategy?

c. What physical resources are needed to accomplish your strategy?

   d. List the cost of each of the above.

3. Finance (Chapter 3)

   a. Additional Funds Needed (AFN). Why does your firm need the cash?

   b. Statements

      i. Balance Sheet

      ii. Income Statement

      iii. Cash flow Projection

      iv. Breakeven Analysis considering AFN

4. Operations (Chapter 4)

   a. List your company's prospective and current contracts. This helps speak for managers when additional funds are required.

   b. List of prospective and current projects. This is important to show that the company can reach for and grasp growth.

      i. Detail your project management style. This is important for companies to show that they have the expertise to drive the organization forward. The United States places heavy emphasis on the

Project Management Professional (PMP) designation. Great Britain seems to prefer PRINCE2 Practitioner. Other nations may have their own preferences for project management certifications. It is important for managers to keep this in mind and source the appropriate talent for their needs.

5. Marketing (Chapter 5)

   a. List the Key Success Factors (KSFs) for your industry.

   b. State the marketing strategy for developing awareness, interest, desire, and action (AIDA).

Have your advisory board look over your business plan. Cook some food, bring them all over your home, and read it to them if possible. You want to present this to a hostile crowd. Your advisory board should not be filled with cuddly friends. If they are normally kind and sweet, they have to have an off switch for that characteristic. Express to your board that you need hard questions that suck the air out of the room. They should not be afraid to be pessimistic about the plans of the company. When you have satisfied their questions, you will have addressed the comments and concerns that may be expressed by others in the future.

Jump Into It

You have read this book. You have developed a plan that considers your industry through key success factors and how you fit through the SWOTT analysis. You are ready. Now bring your plans to life and flourish.

www.ingramcontent.com/pod-product-compliance
Lightning Source LLC
Chambersburg PA
CBHW052347220526
45465CB00003BA/997